Golden Highlights Library

Antique Cars

Lord Montagu of Beaulieu

Camden House Books

Camden House Books
Printed and published by BPCC Publishers
Manufactured under licence from the proprietor

Created, designed and produced by
Trewin Copplestone Publishing Ltd, London

Made and printed in Great Britain by
Purnell and Sons (Book Production) Ltd.,
Member of the BPCC Group, Paulton, Bristol

ISBN 0 905015 07 X

Contents

The author wishes to thank Mr. G. N. Georgano for
the research which is embodied in this book.

Acknowledgements

The publishers acknowledge the research and
photographic facilities provided by the National
Motor Museum at Beaulieu, Hampshire. Black and
white illustrations come from this source, and the
following color illustrations were photographed there
by Tom Murray: 1, 4b, 5, 8, 12, 13, 16, 17, 21, 25, 29,
32, 33, 36, 40t, b, 41t, b, 44, 45t, b, 48t, b, 49t, b, 53,
56, 57b, 60, 61t, b, 64t, b, 65, 68, 72, 76t, b.
The publishers acknowledge the Frank Smith
Collection, Stockport, Cheshire, for the following
color illustrations which were photographed there by
Tom Murray: 33, 41t, 53b.
Color illustrations 24b, 52, 57t, 80t, 80c, 80b were
supplied by Harrah's Automobile Collection, Reno,
Nevada; the color illustrations on page 4 and
the black and white illustration on page 8 were
supplied by Daimler–Benz AG, Stuttgart. The black
and white illustration on page 30 was supplied by
American Motors Corporation.

The Terms "Veteran" and "Vintage" used in
this book originate from the two leading
British old car clubs, the Veteran Car Club of
Great Britain and the Vintage Sports Car
Club. Veteran applies to all cars made up to
the end of 1918, and Vintage to all cars made
from then until the end of 1930.

Title page *A 1925 Bugatti Type 35 racing car.*

The Passenger Car to 1885

L IKE many branches of technology, the automobile had a long period of barely recognized development before a sudden and rapid expansion unparalleled in its social effects. During the thirty years between its commercial birth in 1885 and the outbreak of World War I, it passed from being the unprofitable hobby of a few experimenters to a source of income for thousands, and of great wealth to not a few. Its history, however, stretches back more than a hundred years before 1885, and it is not possible to appreciate the developments of the late 19th century without examining the work of the pioneers.

The first self-propelled vehicle capable of carrying a man was built by an engineer in the French Army, Nicolas Joseph Cugnot, in 1770. It ran on three iron-shod wheels, of which the single front one both steered and drove, and was powered by a two-cylinder steam engine which, with the enormous boiler, turned with the steering. By any subsequent standards, Cugnot's machine had serious shortcomings, such as a running time of not more than 10 to 12 minutes before a halt was necessitated for steam pressure to build up again, but it embodied two essential advances in engineering. Steam engines had been in use for about sixty years, stationary beam engines suitable for pumping water out of mines or for lifting heavy weights, but they had no mechanism to convert the up and down motion of the piston to a rotary motion suitable for driving a wheel. Cugnot solved this problem with a ratchet and pawl mechanism, and also generated steam under pressure which was distributed equally to the two cylinders. James Watt, so often called the father of the steam engine, did not introduce the pressure boiler and rotary motion until 1775 and 1782 respectively.

Cugnot was encouraged in his work by General Gribeauval and the Duc de Choiseul, finance probably coming from the latter who was one of the leading figures at the court of Louis XV. A second vehicle was completed in 1771 and was ready for trials in July of that year. Gribeauval wrote to the Marquis de Monteynard, Minister of War, as follows: "It is proposed to make this test in the Park of Meudon, near the Avenue de Versailles, because a made road is needed, with gentle slopes to ascend and descend, and to enable the driver to gain experience before venturing on to public roads. Further, as the gate of this park is kept locked, we should not be embarrassed by the presence of spectators." However, these trials never took place as Choiseul fell from power and Gribeauval's letter was never answered. The vehicle probably ran in the grounds of the Arsenal where it was built, and it miraculously survived the Revolution, being acquired by the Conservatoire Nationale des Arts et Métiers in 1800. It can still be seen in this museum today. Cugnot was granted a pension of 600 francs a year by Louis XV, which not surprisingly disappeared with the Revolution. Cugnot lived in poverty in Brussels, but shortly before he died in 1804, the pension was renewed by Napoleon. This would indicate that the importance of the self-propelled vehicle was appreciated (Cugnot's machines were intended to be used as artillery tractors), but no further inventors came forward in France for over thirty years.

Opposite *Two views of an 1886 Benz three-wheeler.*

Below *An 1898 Benz Velo 3 hp Comfortable two-seater.*

The first self-propelled vehicle in America was an unusual one. Oliver Evans, a prolific inventor from Delaware, had built a steam dredge for clearing the Philadelphia docks, and as his workshop was a mile and a half from the riverside, some means had to be found to transport the machine to the water. Evans had already taken out patents for a steam wagon, so what could be more suitable than to mount his dredge on wheels and make it move itself? This he did, and the dredge, named *Orukter Amphibolos* (Amphibious Digger), ran on the streets of Philadelphia in July 1805. For several days it made demonstration runs in Center Square (now the site of City Hall), and was then taken to the river where a paddle wheel was fitted, and the drive to the road wheels disconnected. It never ventured on land again, but it has its place in history as the first self-propelled vehicle in the New World, and the first such vehicle with four wheels anywhere. Had Evans received a commission and sufficient backing to build a proper road vehicle he would doubtless have done so with great success. He did build and sell a number of high-pressure stationary engines, and he died in 1819, the same year as James Watt.

From the 1860s onwards the building of

steam cars, or "light locomotives" as they were
sometimes called, became a popular activity
among engineers and inventors, but most
made only one each, and few sold their wares
as they usually retained them in order to make
constant modifications. An exception was
Thomas Rickett, an ironfounder from Buck-
ingham, who sold three cars to members of the
British aristocracy, and one of these performed
a remarkable journey from Inverness to
Barrogill Castle. The owner, the Earl of
Caithness, his wife and a friend sat at the front,
the Earl steering, while Rickett crouched on a
little platform at the rear, stoking the boiler.
During the 146-mile journey the car reached a
speed of 19 mph on the level, and climbed
nearly 900 feet in 5 miles. Rickett offered his
machines for sale at what seems the low price
of £180 each, but found no more than three
buyers.

In 1865 the British Parliament restricted
the speed of self-propelled vechicles to four
miles per hour on open roads and two per
hour in towns.

In France there were far fewer experimenters,
but those who did build vehicles soon out-
stripped Anglo-Saxon design. In 1860 Etienne
Lenoir of Paris patented an engine in which the
piston was moved in the cylinder by the explosion of a mixture of gasoline and air. This
was the first internal combustion engine,
although it differed from later examples in that
there was no compression of the mixture. As
the piston moved forward (the engine was
horizontal) the mixture was drawn in, and at
half stroke was ignited by an electric spark.
The explosion drove the piston to the end of the
stroke, and its return expelled the burned
gases. In 1862 Lenoir fitted his engine to a
carriage in which he made a few short journeys, but a top speed of three miles per hour
was too slow to be of practical use. A successful
internal combustion engined car was not built
until some twenty-three years later, but Lenoir
has the honor of being the first man to use the
motive power which has become universal.

In 1873 Amédée Bollée, a bell founder of
Le Mans, built the first of a number of steam

Amédée Bollée's steam bus, l'Obéissante.

carriages, which he named *l'Obéissante*. This was more of a bus than a car, but it is worth examining because of the progress it represented, notably in steering. Up to this time four wheeled vehicles were steered by a center pivot system, in which the whole front axle turned with the wheels. This was very heavy, and could easily be knocked out of control if the wheel hit a stone. On sharp corners the axle could lock over and capsize the vehicle. In order to avoid this, many builders from Cugnot onwards used a single wheel at the front, but this again resulted in an unstable vehicle. The solution to this problem had been proposed as early as 1816 on a horse-drawn vehicle by a Bavarian coach builder, Georg Lankensperger. His idea was to have a fixed axle, the wheels turning on small stub axles, and this was the system adopted by Bollée, although he had never heard of Lankensperger or his patent. In fact the Bollée system differed somewhat in that l'Obéissante had no front axle at all, the wheels being mounted in pivoted forks, as on a bicycle. The linkage from the steering wheel was by chains, a theoretically sound system which failed in practice because the chains inevitably stretched after a while.

Apart from its steering, l'Obéissante was advanced in that its front wheels were independently sprung (as they had to be in the absence of any axle), it had a full perimeter frame of riveted iron, and an all-metal body. Despite a weight of over $4\frac{1}{2}$ tons, it could carry twelve passengers in addition to the driver and fireman, and had a maximum speed of 25 mph. This was truly remarkable when one realizes that the gas-engined cars on sale to the public twenty years later could not exceed this, even with light two- or four-seater bodies. But excellent though Bollée's machine was, there was no market for it, and within a few years he was to write: "In the end I have come to wonder whether, in the present state of my practical knowledge, I should recommend the use of steam engines." His son Amédée junior built two steam vehicles and then turned to gas, while his younger son Léon made nothing but gas-engined vehicles.

Another view of the 1898 Cannstatt-Daimler 4 hp landaulette seen in the group photograph opposite.

An 1898 Cannstatt-Daimler 4 hp landaulette (top left), a 1905 Rolls-Royce 10 hp two-cylinder tourer (top right) and a 12 hp British

The Beginnings of Production

THE four-stroke internal combustion engine was patented by Nikolaus-August Otto of Deutz, Germany, in 1877, although the stationary gas engine firm of Otto & Langen never made a car. The application of the engine, a vast improvement on the two-stroke engine of Lenoir, was left to Gottlieb Daimler, an employee of Otto & Langen, and Karl Benz, a small-time manufacturer of stationary coal-gas engines. Until 1882 Benz was restricted by Otto's patent to the two-stroke principle, but as soon as the patent lapsed he began work on a four-stroke engine running on gas and ignited by a spark plug fed by a coil and battery. This unit, with single horizontal cylinder, developed less than one horsepower at about 400 revolutions per minute. Benz mounted it in a light three-wheeled frame, specially designed for the purpose, with wire wheels and solid tires. He would have preferred four wheels, but being at that time ignorant of the Lanken-sperger system, the single steering wheel seemed the best solution. This car was tested in 1885, patented on January 29th 1886, and within two years Benz was making improved models with larger engines for sale. His partners in the coal-gas engine business were far from enthusiastic, and had it not been for the support of two new backers, Friedrich von Fischer and Julius Ganss, Benz might never have established serious production. In 1888 he sold a manufacturing license to Emile Roger of Paris, who made three-wheelers at first, followed by four-wheelers. These were sold in Britain under the name Anglo-French, and in the United States under the name Macy Roger.

Daimler driven in the 1899 Paris–Ostend race (bottom right). Inset (bottom left) is the engine of Benz's first car, 1886. The drive is taken by flat belt from the drum to a countershaft, and thence by chains to the wheels.

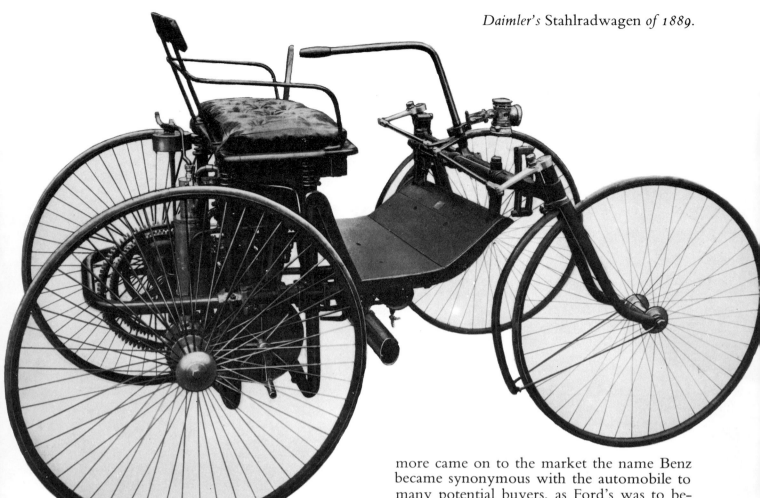

Benz progressed to four-wheelers in 1893 with the Viktoria, a large, cumbersome-looking machine, still with a single cylinder horizontal engine and surface carburetor. Much more significant was his next design, the Velo of 1894. This was a smaller, lighter car than the Viktoria, with wire wheels in place of wood-spoked artillery type, still with a horizontal single-cylinder engine, but with a vertical fly-wheel. The capacity of this engine was 1045 cc, and the power about 2 hp at 600 rpm. This gave a top speed of 18 mph on the higher of the two speeds provided by the fast and loose pulley transmission system. Feeble and slow though it may seem, the Velo sold well for a number of years as it was simple to maintain and operate, and as reliable as any car of that time. Benz production rose from 67 in 1894 to 135 in 1895 and 181 in 1896, most of these cars being Velos. Three years later the figure was 572, which meant that for over ten years the Benz company had led the world in car production. In fact, their 1896 figure was higher than the combined efforts of all the automobile makers in Great Britain and the United States of America. The success of the Benz was, for a time, self-generating, for as more came on to the market the name Benz became synonymous with the automobile to many potential buyers, as Ford's was to become twenty years later. Unfortunately Karl Benz was a conservative character (he was fifty-six years old by 1900) and he refused to modernize his designs until falling sales during the years 1900 to 1903 forced him to hire a French designer, Marius Barbarou, to produce a completely new front-engined car with a vertical two- or four-cylinder engine.

Benz's rival Gottlieb Daimler approached the problem of motorized transport in a different way. His first engine of 1883 was more advanced than that of Benz in some ways, giving $1\frac{1}{2}$ hp from a capacity of less than half Benz's (462 cc), and running at the much higher speed of 700 rpm. It was mounted in rubber to reduce vibration, but on the debit side it used the archaic hot-tube ignition system. Unlike Benz who designed a chassis specially to accommodate his engine, Daimler used a horse-drawn carriage, a crude vehicle with center pivot steering. At this stage Daimler was more interested in various applications of his engine than in concentrating on the automobile, and in fact mounted the engine in a motorcycle, a boat and a balloon in order to test its versatility. His partner, Wilhelm Maybach, was more of a car enthusiast, and in 1889, largely through his persuasion, Daimler built a light car known as the *Stahlradwagen* (steel wheel car), with V-twin engine of 566 cc.

A 1902 Panhard rear-entrance tonneau.

More important than Daimler's cars were his engines which, license-built in France, laid the foundations of the French motor industry. The license was acquired by a lawyer, Edouard Sarazin, who, though he saw the the importance of the internal combustion engine, had no facilities for manufacturing them. To do so, he chose the small woodworking business run by his friend Emile Levassor in partnership with René Panhard. Before any production could begin, Sarazin died. His widow promptly traveled to Germany to ensure that the rights to the Daimler engine were transferred to her, and soon afterwards she married Levassor, thus establishing Panhard et Levassor as motor manufacturers, which they were to remain for seventy-seven years. The engine which was the subject of this license was a V-twin unit with hot-tube ignition and a surface carburetor. Panhard et Levassor mounted it in the middle of the frame of their car, between

A very early mid-engined Panhard, which can be seen at the Musée de la Voiture at Compiègne.

A 1903 De Dion–Bouton 6 hp light car. This was the first exhibit in the Montagu Motor Museum.

the front and rear passengers. The latter faced backwards in what became known as the *dos-à-dos* (back-to-back) position used by a number of car makers up to about 1900. This first Panhard-Levassor was not a particularly significant or distinguished car, but in 1891 Levassor produced a new design which turned out to be the prototype of the standard automobile for years to come. He still used the Daimler engine with its old-fashioned tube ignition and surface carburetor, but he mounted it in the front of the frame, and behind it he installed a four-speed sliding pinion gear system in place of the belts and pulleys used by Benz and Daimler. Final drive to the rear wheels was by side chains as used on many cars up to about 1905, and on heavy trucks long after that. These cars began to be sold to the public, at a price of 3500 francs, in 1891. One of the first to be sold was still being used by a parish priest in 1928! Over the next few years Levassor

made gradual improvements, most of which were innovations at the time. In 1894 the surface carburetor was replaced by Maybach's spray type, and in 1895 the gears were enclosed, thus justifying the term "gearbox" for the first time. The V-twin gave way to an inline twin, still made under Daimler license, while in the cars entered in the Paris-Marseilles-Paris Race of 1896, inline four-cylinder engines were used. These cars also had steering by wheel in place of tiller, as it was found that at speeds of 25 to 30 mph the tiller could easily be jerked out of the driver's hands. There were no racing cars as such at this date, but the latest improvements were usually tried out on the cars prepared for the annual town-to-town races, and later made available in cars sold to the public. By 1899 Panhard's productions had front-mounted radiators and pneumatic tires, and steering wheels, trucks and buses had been added to the range.

13

The Peugeot car christened l'Eclair, *driven by the Michelin brothers in the 1895 Paris-Bordeaux-Paris Race.*

A classic example of the front-engined Panhard, a 12 hp model of 1899.

The other great French *marque* to found its fortunes on the Daimler engine was Peugeot. They were an old-established company who made pepper pots, coffee mills, umbrellas, corset frames and bicycles, and their first experiments in the car field had been concerned with steam vehicles. In 1891 Armand Peugeot bought a Daimler V-twin engine from Emile Levassor and mounted it in the rear of a light two seater with bicycle-type wire wheels. The chassis frame was tubular, and water to cool the engine circulated in this frame, as in Daimler's Stahlradwagen. One of these early Peugeots made the first long-distance journey undertaken by a gasoline powered car, from the factory at Beaulieu-Valentigney to Paris and then on to Brest on the Atlantic coast, as an observer's car in the Paris-Brest bicycle race.

The Hon C. S. Rolls at the tiller of his first car, a 3½ hp Peugeot of 1896.

Armand Peugeot was beaten by many of the cyclists, but nevertheless he earned valuable publicity for the automobile in general and for his products in particular. In 1895 a Peugeot was fitted with Michelin pneumatic tires and entered in the 732-mile Paris-Bordeaux-Paris Race. The Michelin brothers had so many punctures that they used up their entire stock of twenty-two inner tubes, and abandoned the race after 90 hours. Nevertheless, five years later practically all passenger cars used pneumatic tires, although punctures remained the motorists' biggest bugbear for many years afterwards.

Discouraged by the legislation which restricted maximum speed to 4 mph, British engineers lagged behind their European counterparts in inventiveness, which was a sad

contrast to the 1830s when men like Walter Hancock, the steam bus pioneer, led the world. No one in England was foolhardy enough to risk his money in setting up a factory to make cars for sale until after 1896, when the so-called Emancipation Act (strictly speaking the Locomotives on Highways (Amendment) Act) raised the permissible speed for a motorcar to 12 mph. The first company to make cars for sale in Great Britain was the Daimler Motor Syndicate of Coventry whose cars, although they used German Daimler engines, were designed on Panhard lines, with engines at the front, four speed and reverse gearboxes and chain final drive. In 1899 the first four-cylinder British Daimler appeared, and this was also the first of the make to have wheel steering. One of these cars was driven in the 1899 Paris-

A 1901 Lifu, a rare British steam car, showing the boiler under the hood. Note the solid tires, already outmoded by 1901.

Ostend-Paris race by my father the Hon John Scott-Montagu who the same year was the first man to drive a car into the precincts of the Houses of Parliament, also in this Daimler.

If the Coventry Daimler was largely derived from established foreign practice, another British car from nearby Birmingham was wholly individual in design. Frederick Lanchester was a brilliant engineer with experience in the fields of bicycles and coal gas engines, and when he began the design of an automobile in 1894 he worked from first principles, copying virtually nothing from contemporary practice. The single-cylinder engine had mechanically operated inlet valves, hailed as an innovation when used on the first Mercedes six years later, while it was quite unlike other engines in having two balanced cranks, each with its own flywheel and connecting rod. This went a long way towards eliminating the vibration which affected all gas cars at this time, and which must have deterred many would-be purchasers. In-

stead of Levassor's sliding gears, Lanchester used the epicyclic system in which small planetary pinions revolve around a central or sun gear, and mesh with an outer ring gear. This gave easier and more silent gear changes, and also took up less space than the sliding pinion system. The body was a full width affair seating three people abreast, and included a luggage platform. The car was designed to run on pneumatic tires, the first car in the world to be so designed. On the first version, which ran in early 1896, drive to the rear wheels was by chains, but later in the year an improved model with two-cylinder engine drove via worm gearing, again an innovation. Another modification on the second model was the replacement of the tiller by a steering wheel, although Lanchester later went back to the tiller, and continued to offer it as an option until 1911, long after other manufacturers had abandoned it. Altogether it is clear that the Lanchester was a most advanced car, and a refreshing example of what can result when an original mind is brought to bear on engineering problems. Possibly no car made since has incorporated so many innovations as the 1896/7 Lanchesters, and yet the cars were practical too, and within three years a company had been formed to manufacture for sale vehicles which incorporated most of Lanchester's ideas.

Apart from Lanchester one cannot say that there was a great deal of brilliance in the British motor world up to 1900. Herbert Austin designed a three-wheeler for the Wolseley company in 1896, but it was similar to the French Léon Bollée, and neither it nor a more original three-wheeler of 1897 was made for sale. J. D. Roots made a small number of cars powered by heavy oil engines from 1897, and there were a number of British-built

Frank Duryea's first car of 1893.

versions of the Benz such as the Arnold, Liver and Marshall. One Arnold was fitted with the world's first electric starter, a large dyna-motor coupled to the flywheel. This was intended also for helping the car up steep hills or for driving it if the engine failed, but the battery could not provide enough power for the latter purpose.

In the USA numerous experimental cars were made in the early 1890s. The first attested car was a three-wheeler built by John William Lambert of Ohio City in early 1891. He began with a three-cylinder engine, but could not make it work satisfactorily, so removed two of the cylinders, and it was as a monocylinder that the Lambert car took to the road. Lambert intended to make replicas, and produced a catalog quoting a price of $550, but he could find no buyers, and abandoned his work. He did not even establish his right to be considered as the maker of America's first automobile, and when in 1894 Elbert Haynes asked Lambert not to object to Haynes's claim to the title, Lambert agreed. But even ignoring Lambert, Haynes's claim was not justified, for Frank Duryea had a car running in September 1893. Like the original Daimler, this was a horse buggy powered by a single-cylinder horizontal engine. Frank's brother Charles said of this first car, "It ran no faster than an old man could walk . . but it did run." Later another car with a two-cylinder engine was built, and this was followed by replicas made for sale in the latter half of 1895. This made the Duryeas the first motor manu-facturers in the United States. Frank Duryea won America's first motor race, the 54-mile Chicago–Evanston race held in November 1895. The following year the Duryeas built and sold thirteen cars, but after this promising start production dropped to only three in 1897 and in 1898 Charles formed a new company in Peoria, Illinois. He made three-wheelers and later four-wheelers, but the name of Duryea never became prominent in the 20th century motoring world.

While the Duryeas were selling cars a number of other experimenters were putting vehicles on the road, notably Alexander Winton and Henry Ford. Winton was a Scots born bicycle maker from Cleveland who built a 12 hp two-cylinder car which achieved a speed of 33.7 mph at the Glenville Track in Cleveland in 1897. This brought him backing from local businessmen, and in 1898 the Winton Motor Carriage Company was turning out single-cylinder cars for sale. Twenty-two were sold that year, and about a hundred in 1899, making Winton America's largest builder of gas cars up to 1900. Henry Ford's first car took to the road in June 1896, after two-and-a-half years of work. He built it entirely himself, using plumbing pipe for the frame, and bicycle wheels. The crankshaft of the two-cylinder engine was forged by hand. The car had two forward speeds, 10 mph and 20 mph, and no reverse. Compared with many European cars of 1896, which had up to ten years' development behind them, Ford's "Quadricycle" was an undistinguished vehicle, but it is significant as the ancestor of the greatest automotive empire in the world. By 1901 Ford had built three more cars, in one of which he defeated Alexander Winton in a race at Grosse Pointe, Michigan.

The last four years of the 19th century saw an enormous number of car making concerns capitalized in America, and yet very few of them reached the stage of building even one car. Over two hundred companies had been registered by the beginning of 1899, yet production up to that date was little over three hundred cars. The year 1899 saw a considerable expansion, with over 3200 cars made, but the majority of these were powered either by steam or electricity, and will be dealt with later in the book.

Dignity and Impudence

AFTER the pioneer work of Karl Benz and the essential development of Panhard and Levassor, the next really important step forward in car design came in late 1900. Emile Jellinek was the Austro-Hungarian Consul in Nice, a wealthy amateur who, in addition to buying the latest German Daimler cars as they appeared, also acted as unofficial agent, selling to the wealthy international clientele who lived, or at any rate spent part of each year, on the French Riviera. Up to 1900 he had sold thirty-four Daimlers, but he realized that the high, short-wheelbase design was becoming more and more dangerous with each increase in engine power, and certainly for racing a completely fresh design was called for. In 1899 he traveled to Cannstatt to discuss a new design, promising large orders if something suitable could be produced. Paul Daimler, Gottlieb's son, had already designed a small

The 1899 Cannstatt-Daimler 28 hp racing car, direct ancestor of the Mercedes.

car with crankcase and gearbox cast as a single unit, and foot accelerator. This design was improved on by Wilhelm Maybach who worked on it during the spring and summer of 1900. As early as April, Jellinek was sufficiently impressed with what he was shown to place an order for thirty-six cars, a remarkable number when one realizes that it was a totally unproved car, and one which would clearly sell at a high price. However, Jellinek's ambitions for this car extended beyond the confines of the Riviera, for he wanted the sole selling rights for France, Belgium, Austria-Hungary and the USA. In these countries the car was to be sold under the name Mercedes, that of his eldest daughter which he had already used as a pseudonym for himself when he entered races. In fact, this name came to be used for the cars everywhere, and the alternative name of New Daimler never became established.

The prototype Mercedes made its first trials on November 22nd 1900, but some time before this, rumors were circulating about the new wonder car from Cannstatt. In July, Paul Meyan, editor of *La France Automobile,* warned that "French factories would do well to get busy extremely quickly, in order that Daimler should not set the fashion in France". The first Mercedes has been called the first modern automobile, and it certainly incorporated a large number of features which were soon to be taken for granted, especially in high-quality cars of the next ten years. However it did owe quite a lot to its despised predecessor, the short and high 28 hp racing car of 1899, including the honeycomb radiator which replaced the earlier gilled-tube type, the pressed steel frame in place of armored wood, and the gate-type gear change. The Mercedes was lower and longer, making it a much safer car, and also giving it a completely fresh appearance which led to its being called the ancestor of the modern car. The driver sat further back in the

A 1903 Mercedes Sixty, bought new by Harmsworth, and used by him until 1910.

chassis which necessitated a more sharply raked steering wheel; another modern feature was that the radiator was raised so that it was completely framed by the hood, instead of being slung below it between the dumb irons and front springs. The engine was enlarged from 5.5 to 5.9 liters and was given mechanically operated inlet valves with variable lift. This gave greatly increased flexibility of the engine, which ran as smoothly at 500 rpm as at its maximum speed of 1000 rpm. In addition, the gate change with which the driver could change down from top to second speed without having to pass through third, gave further refinement of control.

The new car made its first public appearance at the Grand Prix de Pau on February 17th 1901, but hurried preparation and lack of sufficient testing prevented it from distinguishing itself. The clutch failed and the gearbox jammed within a few yards of the start. At its next event, however, the Mercedes redeemed

itself. The Nice Speed Week included a 279-mile race over hilly country as well as a speed hill climb and a 1 kilometer sprint on the level. Wilhelm Werner's Mercedes won the first two outright, and was the fastest gas-engined car in the sprint. After the races were over Werner's Mercedes was fitted with a touring body, a common practice at this time when the distinction between racing and touring cars was still largely one of coachwork. Jellinek's order of thirty-six cars was quickly sold, although the French agency was acquired by a Paris dealer named Charley Lehmann, and for 1902 an improved model appeared with engine enlarged to 6785 cc. This went up again in 1903 to 9236 cc, the famous Mercedes Sixty which won the Gordon Bennett Race that year. This had inlet valves in the cylinder head, a further advance over contemporary design just as Mercedes' rivals were catching up by offering the 1901 improvements. The Sixty which won the race was an ordinary touring

model lent by an American owner, Clarence Grey Dinsmore, as the special 90 hp cars had been destroyed in a factory fire. This success set the seal on Mercedes prestige, and the cars from Cannstatt soon became world famous, as desirable to the dowager as to the sportsman. An American factory was set up in 1905, at the Long Island City plant of William Steinway, the famous piano makers. It was largely an assembly operation as many parts were imported from Germany. These included cylinder castings which were said to be made from purer iron ore than was then available in the United States. Cars of Mercedes type were also made at the Austrian Daimler factory for several years, until Ferdinand Porsche introduced his own designs in 1910. More important than the foreign-built Mercedes was the influence the new car had on the designs of other companies. Fiat and Itala in Italy, Berliet and Rochet-Schneider in France, Ariel in England, Locomobile in America, all makers of high quality cars, turned out products which followed Mercedes principles to a greater or lesser extent. The major divergence from the original Mercedes pattern was the use of shaft drive instead of chains, which Itala adopted in 1904. The Daimler company themselves adopted shaft drive on their smaller cars in 1905, but continued to use chains on their largest models almost until the outbreak of World War I.

If the Mercedes was the prototype design among large cars for the rich, the middle income motorist owed as much to the De Dion-Bouton *voiturette*. The first De Dion-Bouton gas engine was made in 1894, a tiny single-cylinder air-cooled unit of only 137 cc. Because it knocked badly and the big end bearings failed at its governed maximum speed of 900 rpm, Georges Bouton allowed it to rev up to 1500 rpm. At this speed the explosive pressures were balanced by inertia forces, and the stress on the bearing was reduced. The little high speed engines were first mounted in tricycles early in 1895, and increased in size a year later to 250 cc. The output was now $1\frac{3}{4}$ hp, or 7 hp per liter. This was four times the efficiency of the slow-moving Benz engine, which turned at a leisurely 500 rpm. Despite Karl Benz's argument that the little De Dion engine would shake itself to pieces in no time, the tricycles sold well, and in 1899 the four-wheeled De Dion-Bouton voiturette appeared. This had a $2\frac{3}{4}$ hp engine of 326 cc, soon replaced by a $3\frac{1}{2}$ hp unit of 402 cc. On the early models final drive was to an unsprung rear axle, but this was replaced by the system known

as the De Dion axle. In this, the rear axle was "dead" and did not transmit power; this was done through independent universally jointed half shafts. There was a very simple gear-change mechanism, with a separate clutch for high and low gear (there were only two speeds) operated by a wheel on the steering column. A turn anti-clockwise expanded the low speed clutch to move the car away from rest, and a turn in the opposite direction released the low speed clutch and actuated the high speed one. This made the De Dion voiturette simple to operate as well as cheap to buy (£175) so it is hardly surprising that it became the most popular car made in Europe. The seats were arranged *vis-à-vis* with the front seat passengers facing the driver, which made for easy conversation, even if it seems strange today. In 1902 the engine was moved to the front, under a hood, and the *vis-à-vis* seating abandoned for conventional forward facing arrangement. As on most cars of the period the wheelbase was too short to permit a side entrance for the rear seat passengers, so they climbed in through a door at the back of the car. This arrangement was known as the rear-entrance tonneau.

The single-cylinder De Dion was made in various forms up to 1912, but as it grew more modern it lost its individuality. The expanding clutch was replaced in 1905 by a conventional three-speed mechanism, on the grounds of cost, and the De Dion axle gave way to an ordinary axle in 1909. No design, however brilliant, seems able to hold the stage for very long, and just as Benz grew stagnant and gave way to Panhard, and Panhard to Mercedes, so the De Dion voiturette passed from being the most popular light car in Europe to being one among many competitors, and eventually faded away unnoticed. The company made other cars, including a pioneer V-8, but it can be safely said that their truly significant period was over by 1905.

Out on a Limb

BECAUSE the gasoline-engined car has been dominant for over sixty years it is often forgotten that steam and electricity were at one time not mere eccentricities but serious rivals to internal combustion, particularly in the USA. Of the 4200 odd cars made in the US in 1900, 1572 were electric, and over 1600 were steam cars, mostly Locomobiles and Stanleys. Light steam cars had been built in America since the 1860s, but none of these had been offered for sale.

Meanwhile, in Europe, steam cars were also being built, and although they never became as commercially significant as in America, some important technical steps were taken. In 1883 Count Albert de Dion joined forces with the engineers Bouton and Trépardoux, and the latter built for the Count a series of light steam cars powered by coke-fired boilers. The first had front-wheel drive, by belts, and rear-wheel steering. The second, of 1885, was a three-wheeler with drive to the single rear wheel. Two of these were entered in the world's first motor competition, a short run around the environs of Paris organized by the bicycle magazine *Le Vélocipède* in 1887. Unfortunately only one turned up, driven by De Dion himself, so he could hardly be said to have "won", even though he did complete the course satisfactorily. Later, the De Dion-Bouton company turned out a considerable number of steam vehicles, including the tractor which pulled a four-seater in the Paris-Rouen Trial of 1894, and the brake which won the 1897 Marseilles-Nice-La Turbie Race.

A De Dion-Bouton voiturette of 1899.

The engine of a 1920 Stanley Steamer, showing
the direct drive to the rear axle.

A 1925 Doble Model E, with phaeton body
made by Murphy of Pasadena, California.

A 1920 Stanley Model 735, with British body by Denmans of Cuckfield, Sussex.

The 1924 Doble Steamer looked like a gasoline-engined car until the raised hood revealed the flash boiler. The engine lay by the rear axle.

A Serpollet three-wheeler of 1891 preserved in the Deutsches Museum at Munich.

More significant than de Dion's steamers were those of Léon Serpollet. It was he who devised the flash generator, whereby water was pumped into a multi-coiled pipe, already heated, there to be converted in a flash into superheated steam. This reduced to a considerable extent the time needed to warm up the car before starting it. As there was only a limited amount of water being heated at any one moment the danger of explosion was reduced, although this danger was greatly exaggerated anyway where steam cars were concerned. Serpollet's generator (invented in 1885) was first used in a car in 1887, and in 1890 he and Armand Peugeot built a three-wheeler in the latter's bicycle factory which made a journey from Paris to Lyons, taking two weeks to cover the 790 miles. In 1891 Serpollet put his three-wheeler into production making twelve cars, one of which was exported to India. They had a maximum speed of 16 mph, and could climb a gradient of 1 in 7 fully laden. Their performance was better and more reliable than that of the contemporary internal

combustion car, but when Peugeot withdrew his support because he wanted to make cars of his own design, Serpollet abandoned manufacture for several years. Then in 1899 he obtained fresh backing from an American resident in Paris, Frank Gardner, and in a large new factory he restarted car production. His new cars used paraffin for fuel instead of coke, and were much lighter than the previous ones. The boiler was at the rear and the engine halfway between front and rear axles, the two cylinders horizontally opposed and driving the rear axle by a single chain. A variety of different models were made, from two seaters to large, ornate touring limousines. Racing cars were also made, and Serpollet took the World Land Speed Record in 1902, when a streamlined car nicknamed "Easter Egg" achieved a speed of 75.06 mph at Nice. The later Serpollets were easily the most advanced steam

cars in Europe, with the refinement of a donkey engine or *petit cheval*. This was a small steam engine which drove the proportional feed pump, ensuring that exactly correct amounts of fuel and water were provided. Serpollet died of consumption in 1907, and no more private cars were made after that, although Darracq-Serpollet steam buses were built for a few years, some of which ran in London. Probably fewer than a thousand Serpollet cars were made, but they were by far the most important of the European makes. All the others put together made under two hundred cars.

In American the steam car played a much larger part, and three makes achieved world-wide fame. These were Locomobile, Stanley and White. The first two makes were originally similar, as the designs of the Stanley twins were bought by Locomobile, and also by another concern who marketed the cars under the name Mobile. They were mostly light two-seater runabouts, much less sophisticated than the Serpollets, but also much cheaper. They had two-cylinder horizontal engines driving the rear axle by a single chain, tubular bicycle-type framework, tiller steering and full elliptic springs. Maximum speed was about 25 mph, and once they were running, these light steam buggies had several advantages over their equivalent gas-engined cars. They were virtually silent save for a gentle hiss when accelerating, and they had no gearboxes owing to the extreme flexibility of the steam engine which is as efficient when working very slowly as at higher speeds. Their great drawback was that starting involved a long and complex ritual lasting for at least 45 minutes. This was more acceptable when all cars took time to start, but with the coming of easy starting on the handle and later the electric starter, the steam car was inevitably rejected by the average motorist. As a recent owner, Mr. Paul Woudenberg, said of his 1920 Stanley, "No car could have a bright future whose owner's manual requires, in the starting procedure, that the front carpets, the right seat cushion and seat boards be removed."

Typical of the American light steam buggy at the turn of the century is this 1901 Locomobile.

After 1902 Locomobile turned to internal combustion, and the Stanley brothers brought out a redesigned steam car which was steadily developed over the next twenty years. They did not have the sophistication of the Serpollets or of their compatriots from Cleveland, the Whites, but they outsold all other steam cars for as long as steam survived. In 1906 a special Stanley achieved a speed of 127.66 mph at Daytona Beach, Florida, taking the World Land Speed Record. A year later the same car reached an estimated 150 mph before it crashed. Stanley's characteristic "coffin nose" hood appeared in 1906 and was used until 1915. This hood housed the boiler (Stanley never used a flash generator), while the two-cylinder engine was mounted just ahead of the rear axle. Various models were made, including the delightfully named "Gentleman's Speedy Roadster", a light two seater which came in three sizes, 10, 20 and 30 hp. With the most powerful engine the roadster had a top speed of 75 mph, and some special versions were even faster. F. E. Stanley was once arrested near Boston and charged with speeding at 60 mph. He pleaded "not guilty" and when asked how he could enter such a plea when the evidence was so clearly against him, he replied, "I plead not guilty to going 60 miles an hour. When I passed the officer my speedometer showed I was going 87 miles an hour!" (He was fined five dollars.)

Stanleys were used for commercial work as well as for pleasure. A number of delivery trucks were made, and the twelve-seater Mountain Wagon was a favorite of hotels in mountain resorts. It used the same boiler and engine as the most powerful Gentleman's Speedy Roadster. At least one Mountain Wagon still regularly carries passengers today, at the Magic Age of Steam estate at Yorklyn, Delaware.

From 1918 onwards Stanleys were outwardly similar to gasoline cars, but with increasing complexity came increasing cost. The little steam runabout of 1900 cost no more than its internal combustion equivalent, but the cheapest Stanley of 1918 sold for $2750, when a Ford Model T cost $500 and a Buick less than $1500. From being a serious alternative to internal combustion, steam became the preserve of a dwindling band of devotees, and so it remained until the last Stanley left the factory in 1927.

Several years before the demise of the Stanley, there appeared in California a steam car which excelled all its predecessors and showed the world what steam could do for the automobile if no expense were spared. This was the Doble, in particular the Model E of 1923. Among the innovations of Abner Doble was a really efficient condenser which consumed all the steam generated, and electric ignition which did away with the pilot light and enabled the car to move off in about forty seconds from starting, even at a temperature around freezing point. This was still not as good as a gasoline car with an electric starter, but it was the best that steam has been capable of to date. A flash boiler provided steam to a four-cylinder engine ahead of the rear axle, and performance was really startling. With a light body, an acceleration figure of 0 to 40 mph in 8 seconds was possible, with a top speed of 108 mph. A car such as this was bound to be expensive, but the Doble brothers made it more so by using the highest quality custom coachwork by Walter Murphy of Pasadena. Prices ranged from $8800 to $11200, which made the Doble the most expensive American-built car in 1923. Not more than forty-five were sold over a period of eight years, the later cars being known as the Model F. A number went to maharajahs' stables in India, and among American enthusiasts for the Doble was Howard Hughes who conducted a number of experiments with his own car.

The electric car lacked the exciting performance of steam, but in addition to silence and absence of gear changing it had the advantage of being the simplest to operate of any car on the road. Unfortunately it had one great drawback which has not been overcome to this day; it is not feasible for a normally sized passenger car to carry more than 1600 pounds of batteries, and the power these can deliver is limited. You can have high speed over a short range (an electric car exceeded 65 mph in 1899, but only over one kilometer) or a longer range at a lower speed, although a figure of 50 miles at 30 mph is about the best that can be hoped for. The first electric vehicles to be made in any numbers were taxicabs. London had a fleet of over seventy between 1897 and 1899, and New York had more. At the turn of the century the world's largest builder of electric vehicles was the Columbia Automobile Company of Hartford, Connecticut, who made light runabouts, town broughams, cabs, delivery trucks and buses. Their products were sold in Great Britain under the name City & Suburban, and in France under the name l'Electromotion. A light two-seater was bought by Queen

A 1901 Columbia Electric, formerly owned by Queen Alexandra.

Alexandra, wife of King Edward VII, and used for driving about the grounds of her Norfolk estate, Sandringham. A later owner used the car for shopping when gas rationing was intensified in Britain in 1948.

Columbia went over to gasoline cars in 1907, and thereafter the best-known American electric was the Detroit. This was usually seen as a closed brougham for town use, and was popular with women drivers who appreciated its elegance, simplicity and silence. The Detroit Electric had five forward speeds and the same number in reverse. Operation was by a single pedal which increased the speed as it was progressively released. This pedal was like an accelerator in reverse, and when it was fully depressed the brakes came on. Maximum speed was 22 mph. Most Detroits had small, snubnose hoods, but as early as 1912 some buyers disliked the "old lady" image of the electric, so the makers offered a dummy hood identical to that of a gasoline-engined car. This practice became more widespread in the 1920s, when Milburn and other makers followed suit, but by this time sales of electric cars were down to a trickle anyway. Electricity had no Doble with which to go out in glory, although the Detroit lingered on until 1938, by which time it had a Dodge hood and grill.

Electric cars were less widely used in Europe, and not so long lived, although they were popular for town use up to 1914. In London the Electromobile company rented cars as well as selling them; for £325 per year you could hire a four-seater brougham with all expenses covered except the chauffeur's wages. Open electric victorias were to be seen in the Bois de Boulogne in Paris, and in Berlin, Vienna and other cities. A few French and German companies tried to sell minute single-seater electric cars in the 1920s; these found few buyers, and after about 1924 the only electric vehicles sold were delivery vans and trucks. There was a brief revival of passenger cars in France during World War II, but as soon as any quantity of gasoline became available, the electric car disappeared again.

Cars for the Mass Market

IN 1900 about 9000 cars were made throughout the world, of which 4192 came from the United States. Many firms were still experimenting, but there were enough who were making series of identical designs for one to be able to speak of a motor industry, which one could not seriously have done four years earlier. In the USA steam and electric cars still predominated, but gasoline-powered cars were beginning to appear, in particular Wintons, Packards and Knox three-wheelers. In 1901 there came the first Curved Dash Oldsmobile, and this car soon pushed its way to the head of the US production table, being made in numbers way ahead of its rivals. Ransom Eli Olds had made two steam cars and several electric and experimental gas machines before he turned out the first of the runabouts in 1900 which came to be known as the Curved Dash. It had a large single-cylinder engine of 1.6 liters' capacity and a simple frame with two long springs on either side. These ran the whole length of the car, from front to rear axle, and the center part of each spring served to augment the chassis frame. Like many of the early American runabouts, transmission was on the planetary system, as on Lanchesters, but with only two speeds. Compared with European light cars such as the De Dion-Bouton, the Olds' engine turned very slowly, its maximum speed of 500 rpm being no higher than that of the outmoded Benz, but it was rugged, simple, easy to drive and cheap ($600, or £130).

Before production could begin, a fire destroyed the Olds works including all blueprints, patterns and dies, but one car was saved, and from this new patterns were made and production was able to go ahead. The fire took place in March 1901 and by the end of the year over 400 cars had been made. In 1902 the figure was 2500, climbing to 4000 in 1903, 5508 in 1904 and 6500 in 1905. At a time when many motorists did not venture away from city streets, and when transcontinental runs were the preserve of expensive cars, Olds regularly entered his cars in epic journeys. These included New York to Portland, Oregon (4400 miles) in forty-four days. In 1901 Roy D. Chapin, a twenty-one-year-old apprentice who later became Olds' sales manager and then the founder of the Hudson automobile company, drove a Curved Dash from the factory at Detroit to the New York auto show in Madison Square Garden in $7\frac{1}{2}$ days. This feat, at a time when most show cars were delivered by rail, earned the make great publicity and resulted in an order for 1000 cars from a New York dealer. Not until 1906 did Curved Dash production fall off, by which time the design was old fashioned, and there was strong competition from other makers, including Rambler, Cadillac and Ford.

The Rambler was the product of Thomas B. Jeffery, an English-born bicycle builder whose imagination was so fired by the 1895 Chicago Times Herald Race that he sold out his bicycle interests forthwith and with his son Charles built a prototype car. This was in 1897, but it was five years before any Rambler was sold to the public. Later prototypes of 1901 had wheel steering, front-mounted engines and shaft drive, but Jeffery felt that buyers were not ready for these advanced features and the first Rambler built for sale was a more primitive machine with tiller steering and engine under the seat driving the rear axle by single chain. It was much the same type of car as the Olds, and several thousand were sold between 1902 and 1905 when it was replaced by larger cars.

Above *A Ford Model N, seen with a pony and trap in an English lane.*

Left *A 1902 Rambler Model C.*

*A 1902 Autocar, a lesser-known rival to Olds
and Cadillac. Compare the side tiller steering
column with the centrally mounted one on the Olds.*

Cadillac has been for many years a symbol of luxury and material success, but the firm entered the automotive scene with a light single-cylinder car on generally the same lines as the Olds and Rambler, and selling for about the same price ($750 in 1903). It was designed by Henry M. Leland whose Leland & Faulconer company made engines for Oldsmobile and also for the Detroit Automobile Company, one of whose partners was Henry Ford. In 1903 Ford left to build cars under his own name. Previous Fords, of which there had been several, were experimental machines, but 1708 examples of Model A were sold in 1903, its first year. In appearance Ford's Model A was very similar to the Cadillac, also known as the Model A, and there were design similarities too, in the two-speed planetary transmission and single chain drive. The Ford, however, had a two-cylinder

engine, and for this the buyer paid $100 more than for the Cadillac. Ford was second in the 1903 production "league table", dropped to fourth in the following two years (behind Oldsmobile, Cadillac and Rambler) but in 1906 climbed to first place, a position which it held until 1927. Already Henry Ford knew the way he wanted to go; in 1903 he said, "The way to make automobiles is to make one automobile like another, to make them all alike, to make them come through the factory just alike."

The Model A developed into the Model C in 1904, very similar in design but more modern looking because of the frontal hood. Next came the Model F whose longer wheelbase enabled a side-entrance body to be fitted. The A and C, like many cars of their period, had bodies which were known as rear-entrance tonneaus, the rear seat passengers

climbing in through a door in the back. The Model F cost $1200, and there were more expensive Fords still, including the six-cylinder Model K at $2800 which Henry never liked and which did not sell well, even for a luxury car. However 1906 also saw the Model N, the beginning of the line of development which led directly to the famous Model T. The N had a four-cylinder front-mounted engine, shaft drive and a top speed of 40 mph, but the most remarkable point about it was its price. With characteristic boldness Ford set this at $500, less than half that of the Model F

which had only two cylinders. He was forced to raise it to $600, but even so it was still a bargain, and took the company to the top of the sales league within a year of its introduction. Dealers clamored for the Model N, and were willing to agree to Henry's stipulation that they had to take one Model K for every ten of the popular model that they ordered. There followed two variations on the N, the Models R and S, and then, in October 1908, came the Model T, the car which built the biggest personal fortune ever made from automobiles and which was made until 1927.

As with that other highly successful car, the Mercedes Sixty, the Ford Model T borrowed a good deal from its less illustrious forbears. The four-cylinder side-valve water-cooled engine was generally similar to that of the Model S, with the notable exception of the detachable cylinder head, a pioneer feature which greatly helped owner maintenance. The planetary transmission was also inherited from the S, and was found in quite a number of the cheaper American cars, although Ford's was more silent than most. Ignition was by low-tension magneto incorporated in the flywheel, a feature of a number of European cars but rare in the US. For the first time on a Ford there was left-hand drive; previous Fords, like many other American

cars, had right-hand drive although the rule of the road had always been to drive on the right. The price of a four-seater tourer was $850, and it was this, combined with the reputation for good value which Ford had already built up, that made the Model T such an instant success. Production reached one hundred per day by the summer of 1909, total production for the T's first year being 17,771. Within four years Ford factories were turning out more than *ten times* this figure. This was only possible because of the conveyor belt system, whereby the parts for assembly were brought to the worker on a fixed, timed schedule. Contrary to legend Henry Ford did not invent this system, for it had been used in the Connecticut watch and clock industry for years. Ford is said to have obtained his ideas from the overhead trolleys used by Chicago meat packers.

A 1914 Ford Model T two-seater.

The results of mass production were spectacular, for as the number of man-hours per car decreased, so the price could be brought down which brought buyers flocking to the showrooms, and wages could be increased which brought workers flocking to the factories. By 1916 the car that had cost $850 in 1908 was down to $360, and sales exceeded 734,000 for the year. The process reached its peak in 1923 when 1,817,891 Model Ts were sold, and the cheapest cost only $290. One of the many stories about the T, that you could have it in any color you liked, so long as it was black, arose because of mass production. Up to 1914 a variety of colors was available, but it was found that only black Japan enamel would dry quickly enough to keep the conveyor belts moving at the necessary speed.

The record production of Fords naturally forced their competitors to follow suit, although no other firm was able to rival Ford's success. Even in 1926, the last full year of production, when it was admitted by all except perhaps Henry Ford himself to be an outmoded design, the Model T outsold its nearest rival by more than two to one. Ford's main rivals in the early years were Buick, Studebaker and Willys-Overland. Buick's Model C tourer of 1905 was a generally similar car to Ford's Model F, with a two-cylinder 18 hp engine, two-speed planetary transmission and final drive by single chain. Its main innovation was that it had full overhead valves, a feature of practically all Buicks up to the

present day. It cost $1200. Like Ford, Buick soon turned to four cylinders, although twins were continued until 1911 when a remarkably cheap roadster, the Model 14, sold for only $550. Most Buicks, however, were higher priced than Fords, ranging from $1000 to $2500. Yet in 1910 they sold 30,000 cars, only 2000 behind Ford, establishing themselves as the best-selling middle-priced American car, a position that they continued to hold for many years.

The Overland lay between the Ford and the Buick in price, but by 1914 offered refinements such as an all-enclosed sedan body. All these cars were sizable machines by European standards, robust and capable of carrying five passengers at up to 45 mph.

A 1908 Buick touring, photographed in Mexico. Despite the sizable hood, the engine lived under the seats.

The market for the cheap car in Europe was much smaller than in the United States, and the ways in which makers catered for this market were much more diverse. We have already noted the De Dion-Bouton voiturette, one of the most successful light cars, but there were many imitators. This was made possible because De Dion-Bouton would sell their engines to any outside manufacturer, who could then buy his chassis from another firm such as Lacoste et Battmann or Malicet et Blin and have the bodies built by a local coach-builder. It might be thought that De Dion would have damaged their own sales by this large-scale distribution of their engines (over 120 firms bought them), but their confidence in their own product was well founded, and their rivals' cars were generally less satisfactory and more expensive. Where they did suffer was in the long run, for companies which started with the help of De Dion engines later progressed to more modern designs which eventually stole De Dion's markets. The prime example of this was Louis Renault who abandoned De Dion engines in 1903, turning to four-cylinder units which powered his more expensive cars, and a remarkable 1060 cc twin, the AX which saw the light of day in

1905. This sturdy little car helped Renault sales to exceed 3000 in 1908, and was made until 1914. It was happiest with a two-seater body, when a speed of 35 mph could be held comfortably, but was available as a four seater, either open or closed. With a slightly larger engine of 1260 cc, the Renault was widely used as a taxicab in both London and Paris, some of these surviving in use until the early 1930s. The best-selling British car for several years was the Humber whose first popular model was the 1903 Humberette with 5 hp single-cylinder De Dion-type engine and shaft drive. More than a thousand Humbers of all kinds were made in 1906, and in 1908 they introduced a new light car with a 1½-liter 8 hp vertical-twin engine. This was a sturdy car, but rough and noisy, and was made only for two years. More successful was the V-twin light car of 1912 for which the name of Humberette was revived, which cost only £120 with air-cooled engine, and £135 if water cooling was preferred.

By 1914 the two-cylinder engine was becoming outmoded even for the light car, and there were some excellent small four-cylinder cars available, including the Singer, Perry and Morris Oxford in England, the

Two Bébé Peugeots as entered for the 1913 Cyclecar Grand Prix.

Bébé Peugeot and Charronette in France, and the Fiat Tipo Zero in Italy. The latter was the first example of a light car from the famous Italian firm which had built up a reputation for large, luxury machines in the Mercedes idiom. It had a 1.8-liter engine developing 19 bhp, the four cylinders were cast in one block, and the valves were in the L-head configuration. Top speed with a two-seater body was 50 mph. About 2000 were made between 1912 and 1915. An altogether smaller car, though still with four cylinders, was the Bébé Peugeot. This had been designed in 1910 by Ettore Bugatti who was just establishing himself as a manufacturer in the Alsatian town of Molsheim, then part of Germany. The Bébé had a very small monobloc engine of only 856 cc developing 10 bhp, and an unusual transmission consisting of twin concentric propeller shafts, the outer one hollow, meshing with two rows of teeth on the crown wheel. This gave two forward speeds. It was strictly a two seater, and was only capable of 32 mph, although some were entered in cyclecar races. The Bébé cost £160 in England.

In a separate class below the light cars were the so-called cyclecars which inherited the tradition of the tricars stretching back to the turn of the century. Pure motor tricycles such as the De Dion-Bouton had the limitation of carrying only one person, so the next step, when slightly more power was available, was to mount a passenger seat, usually of wicker-work for the sake of lightness, in front of the rider. This was the cheapest form of family motoring available, and a typical example could be bought for £80 in 1903. Gradually they became more car-like. The rider's saddle gave way to a driver's seat, steering wheel replaced handlebars, and the passenger's seat became more enclosed. The tricar reached the limit of its development in about 1907, after which public demand for better weather protection and for two seats side-by-side eliminated them from the market. The ideal of a really cheap car remained, however, and only three years later there appeared the first of what came to be known as the cyclecars. These had four wheels, but otherwise owed more to the motorcycle than to the car. They had one- or two-cylinder engines, drive by belts or chains, usually wooden frames and cycle-type wire wheels. One of the first, the French Bedelia, had tandem seating with the steering wheel in the hands of the rear seat occupant. On the racing models the man in the

Below *A 1908 Humber 8 hp two-seater. Note the cylindrical bolster fuel tank, imitated from those used on contemporary racing cars.*

Bottom *A 1913 Fiat Tipo Zero with rumble seat. Two other contemporary tourers appear on the opposite page.*

Below *A 1914 Darracq and* (bottom) *a 1913
N.B. (Newton & Bennett).*

front seat also had his work to do, for it was his job to look after gear changing. What had been a trickle of home-assembled cyclecars in 1910 became a flood three years later. By March 1913 over one hundred different models were available on the British market alone. They ranged in price from the £55 single-cylinder single-seater Dew to such comparatively sophisticated machines as the GWK at £135. This was the best-known of several makes to use friction transmission. This involved two discs in contact at right angles, one driving from the engine, the other connected to the wheels by chains or shaft. Sliding the edge of the latter across the face of the former gave a variation of gear ratios. There were four positions for the driven disc, giving four forward speeds. This disc was faced with a friction material such as fiber or cork, and was claimed to last for up to 10,000 miles. In fact, hasty engagement of the discs resulted in "flats" being worn in the fiber, which led to slippage and an unpleasant thumping noise. Nevertheless, friction drive avoided the bogey of gear changing and was lighter than a conventional gearbox, an important point in the cyclecar with its limited power. The standard GWK was capable of 55 mph from its 1069 cc vertical twin Coventry Simplex engine, and had a fuel consumption of 35 mpg.

The GWK was one of the aristocrats of the cyclecar movement, and indeed was considered by its makers to be a light car proper. It is hard to draw a line between the two classes, but the true light car was usually thought of as a vehicle with four cylinders and a conventional drive system. Further down the scale there were many weird and wonderful devices such as the tiller-steered AC Sociable three-wheeler, the Morgan Runabout, also tiller-steered in its original version, and the 4 hp Aviette with a boat-shaped body made of hickory wood, final drive by single belt to one rear wheel, and center pivot steering. The best of the cyclecars gave a good performance for their price, but the worst were mechanical horrors of frailty and unreliability. Curiously, there was a brief cyclecar boom in America, or at any rate a boom in manufacturers, with over one hundred firms announcing cyclecars in 1914. However, in a country where a Model T Ford cost only $440, there was little interest in a cyclecar at $375, which could only carry two people and whose low ground clearance made it unsuitable for all but paved roads which were still in the minority in the rural United States.

The friction drive system, as used by GWK. This is a 1930 model with four-cylinder engine, but the principle is similar to earlier two-cylinder cars.

Cars for the Fortunate Few

THE early automobile has often been called a rich man's toy, and although there were cheap cars as we have seen, the buyer with more than £500 to spend had a magnificent choice available to him. A typical example of a high-quality car at the beginning of the century was the de Dietrich, product of a French company whose origins stretched back to 1769. The 1903 model illustrated is interesting as it represents one of the last of the "pre-Mercedes" era of expensive cars. Its radiator was of the old-fashioned gilled-tube type, very antique-looking compared with the flat honeycomb of the German car, while in the engine the inlet valves were still automatic, and the chassis was of armored wood. It had chain drive, but this persisted on many larger cars up to about 1908. The 5.4-liter four-cylinder engine was based on that used in the previous year's racing cars, as so often happened in the early days of the industry, and gave the car a top speed of about 50 mph, very creditable with a four-seater victoria body. The price of the complete car was £980 which put it near the top of the price league. In 1904 de Dietrich brought the design up to date, with mechanically operated inlet valves and an all-steel chassis.

At about this time car design settled down to a pattern which was not changed radically for thirty years or so. Cyclecar makers might

A line-up of Morgan three-wheelers taken outside the works at Malvern in 1913.

indulge in all sorts of freakish designs, but the quality car followed a layout which was adopted almost universally. This embraced a front-mounted engine, with four or six cylinders mounted vertically, cast in pairs and later in one block (monobloc), a three- or four-speed sliding pinion gearbox at first separate from the engine and later in unit with it, and drive to the rear axle by a propeller shaft.

In 1903 the London firm of D. Napier & Sons introduced a car powered by an engine with six cylinders in line. This may not have been the very first six to be put on the market, but it was certainly the first to sell in any numbers, and marked an important step forward in car design. The large four-cylinder engine might be quite adequate from the point of view of power, but for smoothness a greater number of smaller cylinders was an immense advantage. This process of adding cylinders and reducing the size of each was continued in the eights which came about ten years later, and reached its apotheosis with the twelve- and sixteen-cylinder engines of the late 1920s. Napier's first six had a capacity of 5 liters and cost £1050 for the chassis alone. It still had chain drive, but this was replaced by shaft in 1906 when new and larger six-cylinder cars were introduced. The largest touring Napier ever made was the 90 hp six of 1910, with a wheelbase of 11 feet 11 inches and a chassis price of £1620. A body of suitable luxury brought the total price to well over £2000.

Heavily publicized by the managing director, S. F. Edge, Napiers made a justifiable claim to be the best British cars in the pre-1914 period, and the emergence into the limelight of the newer firm of Rolls-Royce took a little time.

The first car built by Henry Royce in 1904 was a light two-cylinder machine, but much more refined than others of its type. It attracted the attention of the Hon. C. S. Rolls who was looking for a quality car to sell from his London showrooms, and who agreed to take all the production from Royce's little Manchester factory on condition that the cars were sold under the name Rolls-Royce. Up to 1906, four models were made, with two-, three-, four-, and six-cylinder engines. The cylinders were all of the same dimensions (100 × 127 mm), and the cars were known as the 10, 15, 20 and 30 hp models respectively. Many engine parts such as valves and connecting rods were interchangeable, and all except the 15 hp had cylinders cast in pairs. A "Light Twenty" won the 1906 Tourist Trophy Race for four-seater touring cars, and the cars were well received by the press, but they did not attract exceptional attention amid the plethora of makes and models on sale at the time. (*The Autocar*'s table of cars on the British market in 1904 listed over 300 different models.) The six-cylinder 30 hp was the least satisfactory of the Rolls-Royce range, having proportionally less power than the 20 hp, and suffering from the torsional crankshaft vibration that afflicted nearly all six-cylinder engines at that time. The crankshaft was redesigned in the next six-cylinder Rolls-Royce, the 40/50 hp, introduced towards the end of 1906. Other improvements in this engine were that the cylinders were cast in two blocks of three, instead of three pairs, the overhead inlet and side exhaust valve system was replaced by the more modern side valves, and pressure lubrication of the crankshaft replaced drip-feed. The new engine was considerably larger

Left *A 1905 Rolls-Royce 10 hp tourer.*

Below *A 1909 Rolls-Royce Silver Ghost 40/50 hp tourer.*

than the 30 hp, with cylinder dimensions of 114 × 114 mm, giving a capacity of 7036 cc. Power output was 48 bhp at 1250 rpm. The thirteenth car made had a silver painted touring body and silver plated fittings earning it the name "Silver Ghost" which has come to be applied to all the 40/50s. In fact this name is more widely used among present-day historians than it ever was when the cars were new; both in advertising and in press reports, they were more usually called the 40/50.

In 1909 the stroke was increased to 121 mm, giving a capacity of 7428 cc and adding about 5 bhp to the power. This was improved to 68 bhp in 1914, but in fact the question of power output was never of great importance to Rolls-Royce owners, who found that the cars gave excellent performance up to 70 mph with very little gear-changing being necessary. In 1911 a Silver Ghost was driven from London to Edinburgh and back on top gear, returning a fuel consumption of 24.32 mpg. The gearbox had four speeds, with direct third and top being an overdrive, up to 1909, when the overdrive was abandoned, but a return to four speeds, this time with direct top, was made in 1913 after a three-speed car had failed in the previous year's Austrian Alpine Trial. The 1913 Alpine Trial cars dominated the event, although they just failed to win the team prize, and replicas, known as the Continental model, were sold to the public. Although they took part in more competitions before 1914 than they have ever done since, Rolls-Royce cars did not earn their reputation through sport, but on account of their silence, quality of workmanship and ease of driving for their size.

Rolls-Royce's closest rivals among British cars were Napier and Daimler, the latter enjoying the *cachet* of being purveyors of motorcars to the Royal Family. Because of this and the "dowager image" which Daimlers earned in the 1920s, the make has been regarded as ultra-sedate, but before 1909 they frequently took part in competitions, and even built a team of special racing cars for the 1907 Kaiserpreis Race in Germany. These large chain drive Daimlers were not particularly smooth cars, and the six-cylinder models suffered from the prevailing malady of crankshaft vibration. The latter was solved by the Lanchester vibration damper which was, in effect, a secondary flywheel at the front of the engine, while another of Lanchester's improvements was to replace chain drive with shaft and overhead worm gearing. An even more important development, and one which was to change Daimler's image, was the adoption in 1909 of the Knight sleeve-valve engine. Instead of poppet valves which opened and shut with an up-and-down motion against a spring, the Knight principle involved a metal sleeve with ports cut in it, which revolved so that they coincided with ports in the cylinder. The "stroke" of the sleeve was about 1 inch, and they were actuated by an eccentric shaft which, like a camshaft in a poppet valve engine, was driven from the crankshaft. Thus the valves were positively closed as well as opened, avoiding valve bounce. The greatest advantage was silence, and it was this that attracted makers of luxury cars such as Daimler. Knight, an American, promised exclusive British rights for his engine to Daimler, and possibly because Daimler's managing director Percy Martin was also American, the company gave the engine an extensive trial and then adopted it. Poppet valves were dropped in the same year, 1909, and Daimler used only sleeve valves until 1933. Many other firms in Europe and the United States adopted the Knight engine, in particular Panhard and Voisin in France, Minerva in Belgium, Mercedes (briefly) in Germany, and Willys in the USA.

Another alternative to the conventional valve arrangement was the two-stroke principle which was widely used in stationary engines at the turn of the century. The best-known pre-war car to use this was the Lucas Valveless, known simply as Valveless when manufacture was taken up by David Brown & Sons of Huddersfield. The Lucas engine had two cylinders side by side, with two pistons and two crankshafts, and a common combustion chamber. Compression took place in the crankcase, and therefore during the downstroke of the pistons, but before the downstroke was completed the inlet port in one cylinder was uncovered by the other, and the compressed air in the crankcase was admitted, plus a spray of gas, to the combustion chamber. In the earliest Lucas cars there was no reverse gear, for the engine could be made to run backwards by advancing the ignition, but by the time David Brown took over the design a conventional three-speed and reverse gearbox was provided. About three-hundred Valveless cars were made, and the basic design was used in the much cheaper Trojan in the 1920s.

On the continent of Europe there were many firms catering to the luxury car market, and it is possible only to mention a few of them. In

A Daimler landaulette of about 1911.

France Renault made cars right up to the top of the price range as well as their little two-cylinder models mentioned in the previous chapter, and there was also the sleeve-valve Panhard, but perhaps the make which had the greatest *cachet* in the carriage trade was Delaunay-Belleville. This company was well-known for marine boilers, and when they decided in 1903 to enter the motor trade, they engaged the services of Marius Barbarou who had been employed by Benz to modernize their 19th-century designs. Barbarou's Delaunay was a conventional four-cylinder car with pair-cast cylinders and chain drive, and six-cylinder models were announced for the 1908 season. These had more rigid crankshafts than many contemporary sixes, and so were not given to vibration, and used full-pressure lubrication by oscillating oil pump. They came in various sizes, from the 2½-liter Type I, very small for a pre-1914 six, to the enormous 11.8-liter Type SMT, of which only three were made. This monster was built for Tsar Nicolas II of Russia (the letters stood for "Sa Majesté le Tsar"), and although it was quoted in Delaunay catalogs, it does not seem to have found any other buyers. One of its features, which was later offered on more mundane Delaunays, was a compressed air starter which drove a small four-cylinder motor on the nose of the crankshaft. It could also do duty as a tire pump and jack. By 1914, electric starting was being offered. Delaunay-Belleville never took any part in sport, and the great majority of those sold before 1914 were driven by chauffeurs. "No one ever drives his Delaunay" said a contemporary car maker, Fernand Charron, "It just isn't done".

A 1906 Renault 20-30 hp limousine, with British body by Windsor of Hounslow, Middlesex.

A 1910 Valveless tourer. Note the separate screens for rear-seat passengers.

A 1910 Delaunay-Belleville HB6 27 hp
landaulette, with British body by the
Burlington Carriage Company.

*A 1913 Daimler with an unusual owner-driver
saloon body. Most closed bodies on large chassis
were designed for chauffeur drive.*

In America the Mercedes idiom of large T-head engine and chain drive was followed by such makers as Locomobile, Lozier and Simplex, and the latter still adhered to this pattern in 1914, by which time all its rivals had gone over to L-heads and shaft drive. There was no single make which could be regarded as the best American car at this time, although Lozier was perhaps the most exclusive, catering for the same unostentatious wealth as Delaunay-Belleville did in France. Unlike the French firm, however, they went in for racing in a big way, and won the Vanderbilt Cup in 1911. The Pierce-Arrow from Buffalo started as the Pierce Motorette, a little voiturette powered by $2\frac{3}{4}$ hp single-cylinder De Dion engine. This was in 1901, and in 1904 it became the four-cylinder Pierce Great Arrow and in 1909 the Pierce-Arrow, one of America's finest makes. The Model 66 of 1914 to 1917 was one of the largest cars offered for sale anywhere in the world, with a six-cylinder engine of 12.7 liters capacity, and a wheelbase of 12 feet $3\frac{1}{2}$ inches. A feature of Pierce-Arrows from 1913 onwards was the mounting of headlamps on the wings; although this became common with the coming of stream-lining in the 1930s, no other maker went in for

it as early as Pierce-Arrow, and it was a way in which the cars could always be recognized. If they were early with headlamp mounting, the Buffalo firm were the last American company to retain right-hand drive, which they did not give up until 1921.

Although not as well-known as Pierce-Arrow or Lozier, the Welch from Pontiac, Michigan was a pioneer in engine design for it had overhead valves from the first model in 1903. These were inclined at an angle in the cylinder head, and there were hemispherical combustion chambers, a feature not found generally until many years later. The first car made by the Welch brothers, who had a small bicycle shop in Chelsea, Michigan, had a two-cylinder engine, but with the move to a proper factory at Pontiac they turned to larger models, with four- and then six-cylinder engines. By 1909 the overhead valves were operated by an overhead camshaft, a feature which would be used increasingly by European racing car builders in the years ahead, but which was virtually unique on a touring machine. Welches sold in small numbers at high prices of up to $8000, and were supplemented from 1909 onwards by a cheaper car, the Welch-Detroit. In 1911 the Detroit factory

was acquired by General Motors, and unfortunately the Pontiac factory was included in the deal. All the machinery was removed, and used to make a much less interesting car, the Marquette. Perhaps it was poetic justice that this lasted less than a year, although the name was revived for a cheap model of Buick in 1929.

Cadillac added a four-cylinder car to their range in 1906, and from being a rival to Ford in the cheap car class they moved up the market until by 1914 they were in the upper middle class bracket, well below the leaders such as Pierce-Arrow, but in many ways ahead of the whole industry in design. Two examples of this were the introduction of electric lighting and starting in 1912, and of the V-8 engine three years later. Various types of self-starter had been experimented with for a number of years, including the admission of compressed air into the cylinders, or the more sophisticated compressed air motor used by Delaunay-Belleville. In 1911 Henry Leland of Cadillac was experimenting with electricity for starting, and his son Wilfred suggested that the small motors being made by the Dayton Engineering Laboratories Company for operating cash registers might be the

answer. Collaboration between Charles F. Kettering of the Dayton Company (soon abbreviated to Delco) and Leland soon resulted in a starter motor that was more compact than any of its predecessors, and these were fitted to the 1912 Cadillacs. Kettering's coil ignition was also used, and electric lighting completed the system. In one step, the crank, the magneto and the acetylene light were replaced by a unified system still current today. In 1913 an electrically controlled overdrive was fitted. Despite these advances, the cheapest Cadillac cost only $1975 in 1913.

Up to this time no Cadillac had had more than four cylinders, but Wilfred Leland was loath to follow the normal routine of adding a six to the range. He felt that the six-cylinder crankshaft was too long and heavy, and argued that if six cylinders gave the same power with lighter impulses than the four, then eight still smaller cylinders would give still lighter impulses than the six, and because the moving parts would be lighter, higher engine speeds would be possible. The V-8 engine was not unknown, and had been made in small numbers by De Dion-Bouton since 1910, but it was not very satisfactory, giving too little power considering its size. The ailing De Dion

company lacked the facilities to improve their design, but Leland and his team soon came up with a greatly superior V-8 which gave 70 bhp from 5.1 liters. The cars fitted with this engine went into production in October 1914 and sold for $2700. Although not the very first V-8, the Cadillac was certainly the first successful V-8 to be sold in numbers and at a reasonable price. Soon other firms turned to V-8s, notably King of Detroit and Cole of Indianapolis. The latter bought their engines from the Northway Motor & Manufacturing Company of Detroit, who were a General Motors subsidiary and in fact made the Cadillac V-8 engines.

So far no mention has been made of the sports car, for this did not exist as a recognizably separate type until a few years before World War I. Racing cars, designed specifically for events such as the Gordon Bennett and Grand Prix races, had been made since about 1900, but the man who wanted to travel faster than his fellows on the road generally bought a superannuated racing car, or simply used the stock chassis from a powerful car such as a Mercedes or Napier fitted with a light, two-seater body. In 1908 there was held the first of the Prince Henry Trials, an 800-mile event for a trophy offered by Prince Henry of Prussia, younger brother of the Kaiser. The

regulations stipulated a four-seater body and restricted the engine size, and efforts to build the fastest possible cars within these regulations led to the first attempts at streamlining, and also to improvements in engine design. Hitherto the path to extra power was followed simply by increasing the size of the engine, but in the Prince Henry cars of 1908 to 1911 designers almost for the first time set about improving cylinder head design, and making use of lighter parts. Two cars in particular set the fashion for what came to be known as sports cars, although this term was not used until after World War I, the Prince Henry Vauxhall and the Austro-Daimler. The former was developed from a 20 hp touring car of 1908, with a four-cylinder L-head engine which gave about 38 bhp at 2000 rpm. Vauxhall's chief engineer, Laurence Pomeroy, worked on this engine to improve the crankshaft speed, and by the 1910 Trial it was giving 60 bhp at 2800 rpm. A larger engine of 3.9 liters was fitted from 1913 onwards, giving a top speed of 80 mph with a light body. Also in 1913, a few cars were fitted with an even larger engine of $4\frac{1}{2}$-liters capacity, this model being known as the 30/98. Very few were made before the war, but it became the staple sporting Vauxhall in the 1920s.

The Prince Henry Austro-Daimler also

Left *Cadillac V-8 engine of 1922.*

Below *A 1914 Cadillac four-cylinder landaulette.*

appeared in the 1910 event. It was the first car designed for the Austrian firm by Ferdinand Porsche who later added to his fame with such cars as the Mercedes-Benz SSK, Auto Union racing car, and the Volkswagen. Like the Welch, the Austro-Daimler had inclined overhead valves operated by a single overhead camshaft, but old-fashioned features were that the cylinders were separately cast, and final drive was still by chains. This did not prevent the cars taking the first three places in the 1910 Trial, the winner being Porsche himself. They were true sports cars in that they represented a separate line of development from the firm's touring cars, more powerful and more expensive, even though their engines were not as large as the biggest of the Austro-Daimler tourers. About two hundred were made between 1910 and 1914, shaft drive being adopted from 1912 onwards.

Numerous other sporting cars were made in the last few years of peace before 1914. Among British examples were the Crossley "Shelsley" and Sunbeam 12/16, the latter with 3-liter engine developed from that used in the firm's Coupe de l'Auto racing cars. The Coupe de l'Auto also provided the inspiration for one of the most famous continental sporting cars, the Hispano-Suiza "Alfonso". Named after King Alfonso XIII of Spain, who owned several of the cars, this had a rather old-fashioned T-head engine with the long-stroke cylinder dimensions of 80×180 mm. Its sporting appeal lay in its ability to cover long distances at high average speeds, with little call for gear changing. In England the Alfonso cost £545, which was £35 less than the price asked for a Prince Henry Vauxhall. The American sporting car of the period was a less specialized machine, using a stock engine in conjunction with a shortened stock chassis and light, two-seater body. The best-known makes were Mercer and Stutz, the former using a 4.9-liter T-head Continental engine and the latter a 6.3-liter Wisconsin engine, also a T-head. These engines turned relatively slowly, the Stutz giving its maximum power of 60 bhp at only 1500 rpm, but like many American cars of later date they could maintain continuous high speeds. Unfortunately the state of country roads generally prevented them doing so for long, and it has to be admitted that the American speedster was a pretty impractical machine, used mainly for short journeys to the golf links or yachting marina, often laid up in the winter, and practically never used as the owner's sole means of transport.

Above *One of the
very few Vauxhall
30/98s made before
World War I.*

Left *A typical
American
speedster, although
of the post-war
era, the Daniels
Submarine
Speedster of 1920.*

Below *A 1913 Mercer Type 35 Series J raceabout.*

Bottom *A 1913 Vauxhall Prince Henry two-seater.*

A 1912 Hispano-Suiza Alfonso two-seater.

IK-1085

The Vintage Years

WHEN World War I ended there were only 78,000 cars on the roads of Britain, little more than 10% of the number that were running during the darkest days of World War II. There was a tremendous demand for new cars, but the new models which were to bring motoring to a much wider public did not appear for a few years. The first plans to be announced were not for light cars such as the Austin Seven or Rover Eight, but for medium-sized touring cars whose makers envisaged vastly greater sales than the market demanded. The 11.9 hp Bean was made by a syndicate that included two other car makers, Swift and Vulcan, Gallay radiators, Marles steering, and the engineering firm of Hadfields. They aimed to turn out 50,000 cars per year, but their production seldom exceeded a tenth of that figure. Another ambitious firm with a medium-sized car, the Angus-Sanderson, made only a few hundred of them, while the impressively named Motor Manufacturers' Mass Production Syndicate never made one.

The biggest selling car in England in the early 1920s was the Model T Ford, which had been assembled in Manchester since 1911. It was challenged by the Morris Cowley, although at first the high price of the latter was a great disadvantage to sales. In 1921 the Cowley cost £525, whereas the larger Ford was only £195. William Morris, however, followed Ford's gamble that price reductions would bring increased sales, and in less than a year cut the price of the four-seater Cowley to £425, and then to £341. 1921 was a very bad year for the motor industry, but even so, Morris increased his sales from 1932 in 1920 to 3077 in 1921. By 1922, sales were up to 6937. He was greatly helped by a piece of Government legislation which introduced a tax of £1 per horsepower, making the 22 hp Ford much more expensive to license than the 12 hp Cowley. The Cowley's engine was American in origin, for Morris bought it from the Continental Motor Manufacturing Company of Detroit. Continental had introduced their 1495 cc Type U Red Seal engine in 1914, presumably to cater to the American cyclecar makers, for it was too small an engine for the average American car. The cyclecar boom never really materialized, and Continental were only too pleased to receive a large order from across the Atlantic, and quoted Morris a price of only £18. The gearboxes and axles also came from Detroit, so the original Morris Cowley owed a great deal to American mass production methods. It went on sale for the 1915 season, but little over a thousand were made before war production took over. After the war Morris found himself without an engine as Continental had discontinued their small unit, but he was able to have a close replica made for him by the Coventry branch of the French Hotchkiss company.

During the next few years, Morris's price cutting continued, the lowest figure being reached in 1926 when a two-seater Cowley cost only £170. Morris had now overtaken Ford as the leading car maker in England, with 41% of the market. The "bullnose" radiator which had characterized all Morrises since the beginning was dropped in favor of a less distinctive but cheaper flat radiator. This model, with a slightly larger engine of 1550 cc, was made until 1935.

The other name which is always associated with the Cowley among British popular cars of the 1920s is the Austin Seven. Although its sales rivalled those of the Cowley it was in a

different class, being very much smaller. In its original 1922 form it had a tiny four-cylinder engine of only 698 cc, smaller than many of the two-cylinder cyclecar engines of the day, but it was a proper car with four seats and shaft drive. The cylinder head was detachable, it had a mechanical starter, and the 10 bhp engine gave a top speed of 45 mph. The "Baby Austin" was an immediate success, and in 1923 was selling at the rate of two hundred per week. As with Ford and Morris, increased production led to reduced prices, and the Chummy four-seater fell from £165 to £125 by 1929. A wide variety of bodies was available, including a saloon from 1926 onwards which was probably the smallest fully enclosed four-seater car on the British market. A sports Seven was offered by the factory in 1924, but very few were made. The most famous

sporting Seven was that developed by E. C. Gordon England which had a high-compression cylinder head, high lift cams and other aids to performance, and a polished aluminum body with staggered seating. These cars were more suitable for racing than for road work, and each car came with a certificate that it had exceeded 75 mph at Brooklands. The price was £265. Gordon England also supplied a "tamer" sports car for road use, and there were many other firms who sold sporty looking bodies for the Seven. Most of these did not do any engine tuning, so the enthusiast who wanted his car to go as well as look fast bought his body from one firm such as Arrow, Swallow or Cole & Shuttleworth, and had the engine tuned by another, or did it himself.

The Austin Seven killed the remaining cyclecar makers almost overnight, but one two-cylinder light car survived for several years. This was the flat-twin Rover Eight whose air-cooled engine had a capacity of 980 cc, considerably larger than that of the four-cylinder Austin. It was sold mainly as an open two-seater, but four-seater open and closed models were offered, and a particularly attractive style was the two-seater coupé illustrated. More than 17,000 Eights were sold between 1920 and 1925, prices being as low as £145. Later, a four-cylinder water-cooled engine was fitted in the Eight's chassis. A much longer-lived two-cylinder car was the flat-twin 7 hp Jowett, which had been placed on the market in 1913 and which survived until 1939 as a private car, and until the early 1950s in the shape of the Bradford van. Like the Rover, the Jowett engine was a horizontally opposed twin, but cooling was by

A group of British light cars, clockwise from top left: 1922 Rover Eight coupé, 1927 Jowett, 1924 Trojan, 1924 Morris Cowley.

water. The capacity was 907 cc, giving a top speed of about 45 mph. Made originally only as a two-seater, the Jowett was available with four-seater open or saloon bodies by the mid-1920s, and was a substantial looking car considering its small engine size. It was made at Bradford in Yorkshire, and sales were slow to spread to the southern counties of England. A clannish feeling among Jowett owners led to the formation, in 1923, of the Southern Jowett Car Club, which still survives, and is the oldest of the "one-make clubs" which are so popular in Britain today. The Jowett's appeal was that of the purely functional machine which does its work willingly and without fuss, and which is not regularly changed to suit passing fashions. Modern features came but slowly; an electric starter

was not standardized until 1927.

A car with some of the same character as the Jowett was the Trojan. Its design, however, was much less orthodox. The engine was a four-cylinder duplex two-stroke unit, generally similar to that of the Valveless described on page 46. Of 1488 cc capacity and developing only 10 bhp, the engine was mounted under the floorboards and drove the rear axle via a two-speed epicyclic gearbox and duplex chain. To crown the eccentricities, the Trojan's disc wheels were shod with solid tires. The designer Leslie Hounsfield claimed that the long cantilever springs and low speed of the Trojan made pneumatics unnecessary, and pointed to the low cost and long life of the solid tire. An ordinary pneumatic cost about £5 and could be expected to last not more

A 1922 A.C. 11.9 hp four-cylinder tourer.

than 8000 miles at best, whereas the solid cost only £2 and would last for up to 20,000 miles. However, pneumatics were offered as extras from the start, and as the 1920s progressed, more and more Trojans sold were equipped with them. They became standard in 1930, although delivery vans could be had with solids for several years after that. The unorthodox design of the Trojan made it unpopular with garages, and not a few hung out notices reading "No Trojans". The Trojan's specification might remind one of a cyclecar, but it was a substantial-looking vehicle, higher than a Morris Cowley and able to carry four people comfortably. About 15,000 were made before the company turned to a much less successful rear-engined car in 1931. The Trojan was the only car to be advertised in *The Church Times*.

A 1923 Austin Seven.

Among more conventional light cars there was a vast choice available; increased power from a small engine made the light car more attractive than it had been before the war, and the horsepower tax hit sales of the cheaper large cars. Of the makes which failed to survive the 1920s, the best known was the Clyno from Wolverhampton. They were close rivals of Morris in price and type of car, and also in their attempts at mass production. Unfortunately they lacked the capital for large-scale expansion, and their price cutting was a desperate attempt to keep down to Morris prices. The best-known Clyno used a 10.8 hp Coventry-Simplex engine, but a cheaper 9 hp car was introduced in 1928, and this did little good to the company's image. Clyno production ceased in 1929 after about 36,000 cars had been made. The A.C. was a popular light car in the more expensive bracket, made in four- or six-cylinder form. The four used an Anzani engine but the sixes were powered by A.C.'s own engine, an advanced unit with single overhead camshaft and alloy pistons and cylinder block. With a capacity of just under 2 liters, the engine developed 35 bhp and gave the car a speed of over 60 mph. At prices of up to £600 the A.C. Six was not cheap, but its quality and attractive appearance earned it steady popularity, and the basic engine was still in production in 1963.

The 1920s were the heyday of the sports car, and these appeared in every price range. Among the cheapest were the sports Austin Seven already mentioned, and its rival the M-type Midget. This was derived from the Morris Minor saloon with which William Morris moved into the Austin Seven market (and undersold the Seven with his cheapest Minor costing only £100). The original Minor had an overhead camshaft engine of 847 cc, and this was mounted in a lowered chassis with raked steering to make the Midget. The body was a light fabric-covered two-seater with a pointed tail, and there is no doubt that the little Midget had a most attractive sporting appearance, even if its performance was nothing remarkable. Priced at £175, it sold very well, and in its first year, 1928–29, more were sold than of all previous MGs (Morris Garages) put together.

Before the appearance of the sports Austin Seven and the Midget, the small sports car market had been dominated by the French, the leading makers being Salmson and Amilcar. Both began by making light touring cars with four-cylinder engines, a 904 cc sidevalve unit in the case of the Amilcar, while the Salmson had had an 1100 cc ohv engine. Both makers soon turned to the sports market, and keenly supported racing and trials throughout the 1920s. Salmson introduced a twin-overhead camshaft engine in 1923, and retained this advanced layout for all their models, both touring and sports, until the end of production in 1957. They and their lesser-known contemporaries such as BNC, Rally and Sénéchal flourished throughout the 1920s, but barely survived into the next decade. From being the purveyor of light sports cars to the world, France had virtually none to offer, and the young Frenchman who wanted a cheap sports car had to import an MG.

A 1924 Amilcar sports two-seater, with characteristic staggered seats and pointed tail.

5081.

Among heavier sporting metal Britain excelled during the vintage period, the two leading makes being Vauxhall and Bentley. The former announced their new 30/98 during 1919, and put it into production almost straightaway. It used the 4½-liter engine that had been developed before the war in a shortened version of the chassis used for the wartime D-type staff car. It was an excellent fast touring car, capable of 80 to 85 mph if not burdened with too heavy a body, and yet capable of 10 mph in top gear when traffic conditions called for it. An overhead valve engine was introduced in 1922 and front-wheel brakes a year later. The 30/98 remained in production until 1927, when the Vauxhall company was taken over by General Motors, and no more sporting models were made. It never achieved the fame of its rival the Bentley, largely because company policy discouraged racing, but it was highly thought of by owners, and is by vintage enthusiasts today.

The original 3-liter Bentley was announced at the same time as the 30/98, in the spring of 1919, but although a prototype was running by Christmas of that year, the first car to reach the public did not do so until September 1921. It was a more modern design than the Vauxhall, having been designed from scratch by W. O. Bentley. The four-cylinder engine had a single overhead camshaft which operated four valves per cylinder, and developed 65 bhp in the original model. This rose gradually in successive models until 1927 when 92 bhp were available. There were three main variants of the 3-liter, the long chassis Blue Label, short-chassis Red Label, and ultra-short chassis Green Label, of which only fifteen were made. Racing successes came early to Bentley, the very first car winning a race at Brooklands in May 1921. Bentleys were second, fourth and sixth in the 1922 Tourist Trophy, and won the 1924 Le Mans 24 Hour Race. This earned the company, which was still very small, widespread publicity, and the name was taken up by gossip writers and novelists as a symbol of the dashing young man. Prince George, later the Duke of Kent, was an early customer, and colorful drivers such as Sir Henry Birkin and the diamond millionaire Woolf Barnato kept the name in the public eye, so that by the time the 3-liter was replaced by the 4½, in 1927, the Bentley was practically synonymous with the British sports car.

A 1930 MG M-type Midget sports car.

The 4½-liter Bentley was introduced not so much with the idea of increased speed as of greater flexibility. The power output was 110 bhp, but the maximum speed little higher than that of the 3-liter. The engine was of the same design as its predecessor, and still had only four cylinders. A 4½ earned Bentley its third Le Mans victory, in 1928, but Sir Henry Birkin was not satisfied with the car's performance, and suggested that a supercharger might be the answer. W. O. Bentley was quite opposed to the idea of supercharging which he felt was appropriate to small cars with very high-revving engines, but not to the type of engineering to which he was accustomed. If he wanted more power, he would increase the size of the engine, as indeed he had done, in the 6½-liter car which had been in production since 1925. He therefore refused Birkin's request for a factory-prepared supercharged Bentley, but the latter succeeded in winning the support of Barnato, whose money was keeping the Bentley company going. Fifty

A 1931 "Blower 4½" Bentley. The Amherst Villiers supercharger can be clearly seen in front of the radiator.

supercharged cars, or "Blower 4½s" as they were familiarly called, were made, as well as four racing models which were assembled at the premises of a rich friend of Birkin's, the Hon. Dorothy Paget. The supercharger was designed by Charles Amherst Villiers, and boosted power and speed from 110 bhp at 3500 rpm to 240 at 4200. It was perhaps rather naïve to expect that such increases could be obtained without reliability problems arising, and in fact none of the blown cars won a race. The general pattern was to set an extremely high speed for a few laps, often breaking the lap record, and then to retire, usually with bearing failure. Heavy fuel consumption and rapid destruction of spark plugs prevented the cars being very popular among road-going motorists, added to which the supercharger was really only happy when operating at constant speeds. Its greatest achievement was to break the Brooklands Outer Circuit Lap Record, at 137 mph, appropriately with Birkin at the wheel.

The very antithesis of Bentley's philosphy was that of Ettore Bugatti who built jewel-like small racing and sports cars which were often fitted with superchargers from 1924 onwards. The first post-war Bugatti was the Brescia, a 1.4-liter four-cylinder car developed from the pre-war Type 13. In 1922 came Bugatti's first production straight-8, the Type 30. It had a 2-liter engine with single overhead camshaft and three valves per cylinder. For the first time, front wheel brakes were provided on a Bugatti. The Type 30 was not particularly successful, but is important in that it was the precursor of the Type 35, one of the most successful racing cars ever made. It was also one of the most beautiful, with a slim body and pointed tail which were the essence of functional design. When it first appeared at the 1924 French Grand Prix it was an unsupercharged 2-liter straight-8, but later versions had smaller engines and superchargers, while the final Type 35B had a 2.3-liter supercharged engine. It is impossible to chronicle all the racing successes of the Type 35, but in 1926 alone the model won twelve major Grands Prix, in addition to countless smaller events and hill climbs. A total of three hundred and forty were made between 1924 and 1930, a remarkable total for a car which was much more a racing than a sports car, although some were driven on the road in the days when police, particularly in France, were less fussy about fenders and mufflers. This also applied to the four-cylinder 1½-liter Type 37.

Bugatti's main rival on the Grand Prix circuits during this period was Alfa Romeo who also made very fine sports cars. In 1925 a new designer, Vittorio Jano, joined the company, and as well as the P2 Grand Prix car he produced the first of a new line of road-going cars, the Tipo 6C. This light and elegant looking sports car had a 1½-liter six-cylinder single overhead camshaft engine developing 44 bhp and giving a top speed of 68 mph. In 1928 a new model called the Gran Turismo with twin overhead camshaft engine joined the range, and in supercharged form won many races including the thousand-mile road race known as the Mille Miglia and the Belgian 24 Hour Race at Spa. The engine was enlarged to 1752 cc in 1929, and this model, known as the 1750, was even more successful than its predecessor. In 1931 the range was extended still further, with the 8C 2300, a 2.3-liter twin-cam straight-8 which developed 130 bhp at

The monocoque frame of the 1922 Lancia Lambda.

4900 rpm. It was made in three chassis lengths, and when the shortest of these, the 8 feet 8 inches Monza, was fitted with a light body, its performance was close to that of the Grand Prix car which in fact used an enlarged version of the 2.3-liter engine. Even with the long chassis, a top speed of 105 mph was possible, a very high figure for 1931 when many small family cars were hard put to it to reach half this speed. Naturally, such a car was expensive to make, and even at a selling price of £1725 the firm barely made a profit. A total of 188 8Cs were made, from 1931 to 1934.

Among Italian touring cars, Fiat was the largest producer by far, just as it is today, with a range during the 1920s that ran from a 990 cc light car, the 509, up to an enormous 6.8-liter V-12 of which only ten were made. More significant in design than any of the Fiats was the Lancia Lambda, which was one of the very few radically new cars that was also

commercially successful. Vincenzo Lancia was a successful racing driver for Fiat who turned to building good quality cars in 1906. They showed no signs of unconventional thinking at first, but during World War I Lancia turned to the idea of a V-engine, but with a narrower angle between the cylinders than the 90° of the Cadillac. In 1919 Lancia showed a V-12 engine whose cylinder angle was only 22°, which allowed for monobloc casting instead of two banks of cylinders. This did not go into production, but in 1921 there came the 4.6-liter V-8 Trikappa, and at the same time Lancia was working on a narrow V-4 engine to power a cheaper car than he had yet made. His new design also embraced independent front suspension by sliding pillars and vertical coils, and did away with the conventional chassis. Instead Lancia designed a monocoque hull built up from hollow steel pressings which combined the frame with the lower half of the body; the seat squabs acted as cross members of the frame. At 2352 lb this weighed much less than a conventional chassis of this size of car. This 2.1-liter car was christened the Lambda, went into production in 1923 and remained in the Lancia range until 1931, by which time over 13,000 had been made. For most of this period it was the only Lancia model. It had excellent road-holding, and came to be thought of as a sports car in England, although in its native Italy it was simply a good fast tourer. Many of the later saloons were used as taxicabs.

In the luxury car market Rolls-Royce came to be more important than it had been before the war, although the Silver Ghost was little changed, and by the time of its replacement in 1926 it was distinctly old-fashioned. The main improvement in the Ghost's last years was the adoption of front-wheel brakes in 1924. It was replaced by the New Phantom, or Phantom 1 as it has since come to be known. This had a larger six-cylinder engine of 7668 cc, built in two blocks of three, with a common detachable head. In response to criticisms of its predecessor's brakes, it had mechanical servo brakes of the type that its rival Hispano-Suiza had used since 1919. The chassis cost £1850, and the price of a complete car ranged from £2602 for a tourer to £2932 for a sedanca de ville. A special body could cost still more, and no Rolls-Royce was supplied with a body by the factory. Like its predecessor, the Phantom was made in America where the favorite coachbuilder was Brewster. A total of 2200 chassis left the British works, and 1240 left the American works.

A 1925 Rolls-Royce Phantom 1 tourer.

The car which many people thought superior to the Rolls was the Hispano-Suiza. The pre-war Alfonso sports car was not continued, and the Spanish factory made a range of not very exciting touring cars, but from the new factory at Bois-Colombes near Paris there came the H6, a superbly modern luxury car powered by a 6.6-liter single overhead camshaft six which gained much from the lessons the company had learned making airplane engines during the war. In its original 1919 form it developed 135 bhp compared with the Silver Ghost's 80, and four-wheel servo brakes were standard from the start. Although made in smaller numbers than the Rolls, the Hispano soon acquired a glamor particularly associated with the Bright Young People and the slightly raffish life of the French Riviera. It was the car driven by the heroine of that extremely popular novel by Michael Arlen, *The Green Hat,* and this brought it to the notice of many people who might never see a Hispano, let alone own one. An 8-liter model was added to the 6½ in 1924, and the two made side-by-side until 1931, when a smaller 4.6-liter six and a larger 9.4-liter V-12 came into the range. The latter cost £2500 for the chassis alone.

Italy's equivalent of the Rolls and Hispano-Suiza was the Isotta-Fraschini which was one of the pioneers of the straight-8 engine. The aluminum block was a single casting, and the heads were in two groups of four. The original Tipo 8 had a capacity of 5.9 liters, but in 1924 it was replaced by the Tipo 8A with a considerably larger engine of 7.3 liters. This was intended to meet the competition provided by the 8-liter Hispano-Suiza, but the Isotta was never such an attractive car, particularly to the owner driver. Quite a number were sold on the American market, where prices ran as high as $22,500.

In Germany there was no rival to the Mercedes (Mercedes-Benz after 1926) either in the luxury or sporting world. The early post-war Mercedes were rather clumsy-looking cars with angular bodies and the pointed V-radiator that characterized practically every German car from about 1914 to 1925. This uniformity of design is a curious feature, for whereas almost all of the seventy or so Teutonic makes had V-radiators in 1923, they had nearly all gone over to flat radiators two years later. The larger Mercedes were exceptions, and the famous K and later S series retained the V design until production ended in 1933. These cars were designed by Ferdinand Porsche who joined the Stuttgart firm shortly before they amalgamated with their old rivals, Benz. The engine was a single overhead camshaft six with vertical valves, originally of 6240 cc capacity (the Type K), and successively enlarged to 6789 cc (Type S), and 7020 cc (Types SS, SSK and SSKL). The K could be had with a variety of bodies from sports

tourer to limousine, but its brakes prevented it from being a serious competition car. Its successor the S was a lower and better-looking car, and the extra power (180 bhp) was restrained by larger brake drums. It was much more of a sports car and very few were made with closed bodywork. This applied even more to its successor the SS which was announced in 1928. The engine of this model developed 170 bhp, or 225 bhp when supercharged, and the car came in two wheelbase lengths, the 11 feet 2 inches SS and the 9 feet 8 inches SSK. The latter was the epitome of the German sports car in the same way that the Blower 4½ Bentley typified its British equivalent. Its aggressive V-radiator and the banshee wail of its supercharger gave it tremendous appeal to enthusiasts, and it had a very fine competition record. The most successful driver was Rudolf Caracciola who won the 1929 Tourist Trophy, 1930 Irish Grand Prix and 1931 German Grand Prix in these cars. Its final development, the SSKL, developed 300 bhp and had a maximum speed of 147 mph. This was strictly a competition car, and only five were made.

Austria's best-known sporting car, the Austro-Daimler, could be said to be a distant cousin of the Mercedes, for both were descended from the original Mercedes of 1901, and both were designed by Ferdinand Porsche.

The superb Model H6 Hispano-Suiza, with an English body by the Grosvenor Carriage Company.

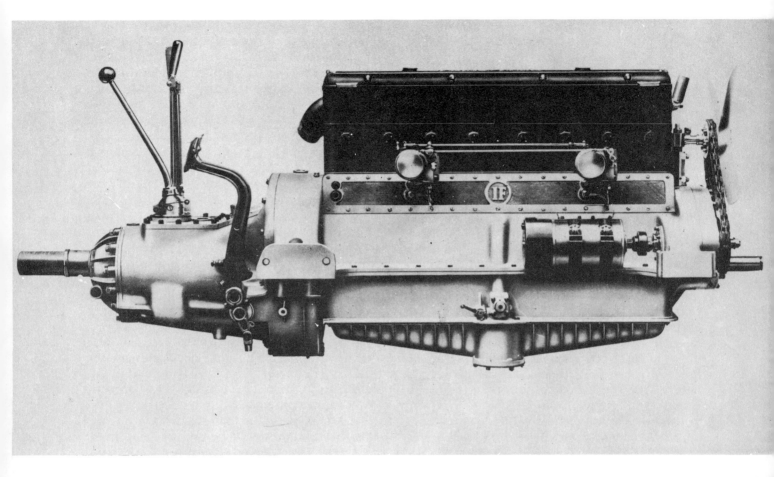

The ADM was a high-quality fast tourer in the same class as the 3-liter Bentley, although with a smaller engine of 2650 cc. Like the Bentley, the six cylinders had overhead valves actuated by a single overhead camshaft. Later developments of the Austro-Daimler, after Porsche had left the firm, had a very advanced chassis which consisted of a tubular backbone enclosing the propeller shaft, forked at the front to carry the engine. Rear suspension was independent by swinging half axles. This layout of tubular backbone frame and independent rear suspension was adopted by a number of manufacturers in Austria, Germany and Czechoslovakia.

Top *Straight-8 engine of the Isotta-Fraschini Tipo 8A.*

Top right *A 1925 Isotta-Fraschini Tipo 8A with sports body by Will Short of Winchester, England.*

Right *Closed coachwork was rare on the Mercedes-Benz Type S, but this one carries a handsome Weymann four-door saloon body.*

A *1927 Lancia Lambda and a 1933 Alfa-Romeo*
8C 2300, the latter once owned by Mike
Hawthorn and regularly used by him on the road.

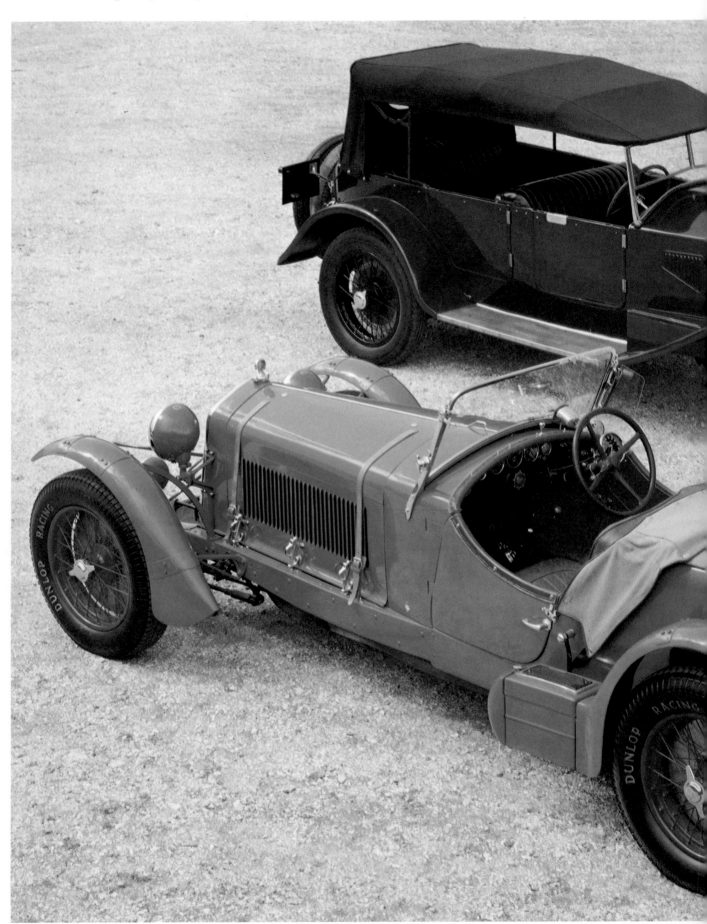

In America the automobile occupied a very different place from that in any European country. At the end of the war there was one car for every twenty-seven inhabitants, compared with one for every one hundred and eighty in Great Britain, and one per thousand in Italy. For Americans the car was no longer a luxury or a status symbol, and the two-car family was beginning to appear. This was largely due to Ford, and during the early 1920s production of the Model T reached new heights, with over 1,817,000 being made in 1923. During the decade, Ford's rivals began to claim an increasing share of the market and the most important of these rivals was Chevrolet. This was the product of that great entrepreneur Billy Durant and the racing driver Louis Chevrolet. The make began in 1911 as a not particularly distinguished, medium-priced six-cylinder car. In 1915, however, Durant launched a direct attack on the Ford market with the Chevrolet 490. This had a four-cylinder 2.7-liter overhead valve engine, and was named after its price of $490. This was the same as the 1915 Ford, but by the time the Chevrolet was put on the market, in October, Ford had cut his price to $440. Durant made several more price slashes in response to Ford's moves, but he was never able to undercut his rival. However, the 490 set Chevrolet on the road to mass production, and from tenth place in the 1915 sales charts the company rose to second in 1919. There was a very low-priced V-8 in 1918 at $1100, and an air-cooled four in 1923, but Chevrolet found that standardization on one model was the best policy for a large-production firm. The 490 was replaced by the Superior in 1922, a more modern-looking car but still using the old engine which in fact soldiered on until 1928 when Chevrolet abandoned fours and launched the International Six, a 3.2-liter car with front-wheel brakes. Though bodies were changed out of all recognition over the years, the International Six engine remained unaltered except for a slight enlargement until 1953. From 1922 through 1926 Chevrolet remained in second place behind Ford, but in 1927 they leapt ahead and remained in first place.

The reason for Ford's slip in 1927 was that the factories were idle for six months during the change over from the Model T to its successor the Model A. For a firm of Ford's size to suspend production of a car with which a whole generation had grown up, not only buyers but workers as well, and replace it with a completely new model, was a traumatic experience.

Nevertheless, Ford agents ordered 375,000 of the new car before they even knew its specifications, and such was the secrecy that surrounded the A that they had to wait several months before they knew what sort of car they were going to have to sell. For those who expected something earth-shattering and ultra-modern the A was a disappointment, for its appearance, though an improvement on the T, was still rather short and high for its date, the engine was only a four-cylinder one, and the T's transverse suspension was retained. The planetary gearshift was replaced by a conventional three-speed system with central lever. The greatest asset of the Model A was its performance, for with 40 bhp and a weight of only 2548 lb even for a sedan it could out-accelerate many cars costing twice as much. Model A prices started at $450 for a two-seater roadster, and ran up to $1200 for a town car of which very few were sold. In 1929 the first mass-produced station wagon was launched by Ford on the A chassis.

A 1922 Chevrolet Model FB touring car.

A *1931 Ford Model A Victoria with many
extras including chromed spare wheel cover and
detachable trunk.*

*Four Model As being delivered to the dealer by
Model AA articulated Ford truck.*

Opposite top *A 1920 Opel 8/25PS tourer, with typically Germanic V-radiator.*

Left *A 1925 Austro-Daimler Model ADM/BK tourer*

Above *Two views of a 1929 Mercedes-Benz SSK supercharged coupé, with coachwork by Corsica.*

Among Ford's rivals in the cheap car market, one of the most successful was the Overland Four, the cheapest car made by the Willys Overland Corporation whose larger products used sleeve valve engines. The Overland was a similar type of car to the Chevrolet 490, although the 2.9-liter four-cylinder engine had side valves. Prices ranged from $595 for a tourer to $1575 for a boxy-looking four-door sedan which, nevertheless, sold remarkably well. By 1925 the price of a two-door coach sedan was down to $495. The same year there came an even smaller four, the Whippet, with an engine of only 2.2 liters capacity.

In a higher price category, one of the outstanding American cars of the 1920s was the Chrysler. Walter P. Chrysler had worked for Buick and Willys (he was reputedly paid one million dollars a year to re-organize Willys), and in 1923 he took over the Maxwell company with the object of producing a car which would incorporate the ideas he had dreamed of while working for other people. He wanted to build a car "with the power of a super-dreadnought, but with the endurance and speed of a fleet scout cruiser . . .". When the Chrysler Model 70 emerged at the end of 1924 it was seen to be a handsome looking car with a six-cylinder 3.2-liter engine which

developed a remarkable 70 bhp. Unlike many cars which were adapted for them, the Chrysler was designed with front-wheel brakes in mind, and hydraulic ones at that.

The trend to increased number of cylinders was more marked in America than anywhere else, and hard on the heels of the Cadillac V-8 came Packard's V-12 in 1915. The Twin Six, as it was called, had a capacity of 6950 cc and developed 88 bhp. As well as being the first twelve-cylinder car to be sold to the public, it pioneered the use of aluminum pistons in American touring cars, and led to the development of Liberty airplane engines. Prices started at $2600 which was not expensive for a large, luxury car, and over 35,000 were sold in seven seasons. In the same month as the Packard there was announced another twelve-cylinder car, made by the National Motor Car Company of Indianapolis. This had a comparatively small engine of $5\frac{1}{2}$-liters, later enlarged to 6 liters. The latter unit developed 82 bhp, and prices ran from $1990 to $3750. The National V-12 was made until 1920, and in the meantime a whole crop of American V-12s appeared. At least twelve other firms announced such cars, many of them using a proprietary engine made by Weidely.

The V-8 was even more common, and

although Chevrolet's was short-lived, several other manufacturers in the medium-priced class used this layout. Oldsmobile made a side valve V-8 from 1916 to 1923 which sold for as little as $1295 in its cheapest form, while among more expensive cars there was Henry Leland's Lincoln, taken over by Ford in 1922, the Peerless, the Cunningham, and, of course, Cadillac, who made V-8s continuously from 1915 to the present day. An attractive small production V-8 was the Wills Sainte Claire, designed by Childe Harold Wills who had previously worked for Ford. His engine was unusual in that it used two overhead camshafts, one to each bank of cylinders, instead of a single shaft in the hollow of the V as most other V-8s did at this time. The engine was quite small, just over 4 liters, and it did not have a high performance, but it was beautifully made and the car was good value at $2475.

Among straight-8s, the Packard was one of the most respected, but for glamor no car could touch the Duesenberg. This company made the first straight-8 engine to be sold to the public, in 1921, derived from their racing engine. The 4.2-liter single overhead camshaft unit developed 90 bhp, and another pioneer feature was the use of hydraulic brakes on all four wheels. This Duesenberg Model A was made in small numbers until 1926, and although a pioneer design, it did not attract a great deal of attention among the many luxury cars on the market at the time. In 1926 the Duesenberg company came under the control of Erret Lobban Cord, a dynamic young man who had already re-vitalized the Auburn company and who gave Fred Duesenberg a free hand in designing a new car which would be the finest in America. The result was the Model J which appeared at the end of 1928. Its engine was a straight-8 with twin overhead camshafts, a feature previously seen only on a few high performance European cars, and never on an engine as large as the Duesenberg's. This combination of size (6.8 liters) and advanced design resulted in the vast power of 265 bhp, at a time when 100 bhp was a very respectable figure. Top speed was 116 mph, and 89 mph was attainable in second gear. Naturally such a car could not be cheap, but in the heady pre-Depression atmosphere of early 1929, Cord was not worried about matters of price. The Model J chassis cost $8500, and the addition of a suitable body brought the final price to anything between $13,000 and $19,000. One or two very special cars, such as the 178-inch wheelbase "throne car" built for Father Divine, cost up to $25,000. About four hundred and seventy examples of the Model J, and its supercharged variant the SJ, were made between 1929 and 1937. Not more than ten were sold in England, and about twenty in France where some of the leading coachbuilders furnished some magnificent bodies. One of these, built by Fernandez for Greta Garbo, was recently sold at auction in the United States for $90,000. Among other owners of Duesenbergs were Clark Gable, Gary Cooper, Mae West, Elizabeth Arden, Marion Davies and Mayor Jimmy Walker of New York. The Duesenberg was conceived during an era of boom but had to struggle for its sales during the worst depression the 20th century has known.

The decade 1920 to 1930 had seen steady rather than spectacular progress in car design, but the spread of features like electric starters and interior heaters to modestly-priced cars meant more to the average motorist than twin camshafts and superchargers. In Europe especially, the family car of 1930 was a far more practical vehicle for comfortable travel in all weathers than its predecessor, and among expensive cars the turn of the decade represented a peak in quality and beauty of design which many think has never been surpassed.

Below *A 1922 Wills Sainte Claire Model A-68 roadster, and (center) a 1929 Ford Model A cabriolet.*

Bottom *A 1929 Duesenberg Model J with convertible roadster body by Murphy of Pasadena, California.*